The Steal—V
The Cover-up

The Steal—Volume III: The Cover-Up

Zero Enforcement, Evidence Ignored, The Courts, Jan 6, The Audits, Hunter Biden's Laptop, The Censorship Complex, The Non-Election System Secret, and What's Next

Joe Hoft

ISBNs: 9798399913681

Dedication

This book is dedicated to President Trump and the record-setting tens of millions of men and women who voted for him in the 2020 Election.

As I mentioned in *The Steal – Volume II: The Impossible Occurs*, Americans risk shame, attacks, frivolous lawsuits, and imprisonment to get to the truth about the 2020 Election. Despite Big Media and Big Tech pushing lies and censoring Americans who stand up and speak about the steal, this doesn't change the facts.

Political leaders from both parties, the Department of Justice, and the courts refused to address the clear evidence of fraud embedded in the 2020 Election, but Americans know what they saw and have never wavered.

President Trump shared with me this short message after I sent him a copy of my first book in this series, *The Steal - Volume I: Setting the Stage*:

> Thank you for sending a copy of your book, *The Steal - Volume I: Setting the Stage*. It is straightforward and accurate—we won and they know it.
>
> I look forward to the next volume. Keep up the great work!

I again worked diligently to keep this book as straightforward and accurate as the first two books in this series.

Based on my professional opinion, these three books in *The Steal* series provide more than enough evidence to prove that the 2020 Election results were not accurate and the processes that led to its results were not transparent, fair, or just. Finally, as noted in the following pages in this book, the efforts to cover-up the many discrepancies that made the 2020 Election uncertifiable were monumental.

The 2020 Election should have never been certified, and as a result, the 2020 Election was stolen from President Trump and America.

CONTENTS

ACKNOWLEDGMENTS

MANY THANKS TO President Trump, who showed us all what courage really is. He stood up and spoke the truth, despite the many lies from Big Media, Big Tech, foreigners, Democrats, and even some Republicans. He spoke the truth no matter what they claimed and did what he knew was best for the country in the face of constant attacks.

Who can even imagine what it must be like to know in your heart that you won the Presidential race and that it was taken from you? President Trump continued to speak the truth about the stolen election, even though the media and politicians claimed otherwise and labeled him a sore loser.

These same scoundrels then attempted to pin the Jan 6 riot on him. Fortunately, no one is buying the lies from Big Media and corrupt politicians in both parties. Americans knew the election was stolen and never gave up demanding the truth.

Special thanks to all those who assisted in putting this manuscript together, especially my twin Jim. This book wouldn't have been completed if *The Gateway Pundit* hadn't had the courage to report the truth on the election while accumulating the largest inventory in existence of articles about the stolen 2020 Election.

Finally, thanks to the many Americans who never gave up. You knew "The Steal" occurred, and you were determined to get to the truth. Thanks to you, America has hope for a great future.

1

INTRODUCTION

(**THIS BOOK TAKES off where *The Steal – Volume II: The Impossible Occurs* left off.)**

In God's time not mine. Due to multiple opportunities, tasks, and other opportunities since the publication of the second book in this series – The Steal - Volume II: The Impossible Occurs *– the final draft of this book was not complete until early May 2023. This turned out to be a good thing.*

Since the 2020 Election, there has been little written about how the election was stolen. In The Steal - Volume I: Setting the Stage, *the many activities leading up to the 2020 Election related to the election were described. In that volume, the efforts by Big Media and Big Tech were discussed, along with how they colluded against President Trump. What we didn't know then that we know today is that Big Tech was colluding with the FBI, and US and foreign governments in a sophisticated manner never imagined. This is discussed in the chapter about the censorship-industrial complex.*

Another observation that became apparent in the writing of this book was the amount of effort, resources, and money that was spent covering up the stolen 2020 Presidential election.

What you can see when reading this book is that a large piece of the 2020 Election steal occurred after the steal took place. Bad actors covered up the steal and claimed that the election was fine and "the most secure election in US history."

This was a lie. The 2020 election steal is arguably the greatest crime committed against this country in its nearly 250-year existence. The COVID catastrophe and the reaction to it and the Russia collusion lie are two other recent major crimes against the citizens of the United States of America. All three of these crimes are connected.

After completing this third book in The Steal *series, I am even more convinced that:*

The 2020 Election should have never been certified, and as a result, it was stolen from President Trump and America.

President Trump's popularity grew over his four years in office. Americans saw how their pocketbooks were growing and loved it. Whatever the left tried to throw at President Trump, it didn't stick. His numbers grew. This showed in the tens of thousands of rallygoers who showed up at his many rallies leading up to the 2020 Election.

In *The Steal – Volume I: Setting the Stage*, a comparison was made between the number of individuals at President Trump's rallies between Labor Day and Election Day in 2020 compared to Biden's totals during the same time period. The difference was startling. As explained in *The Steal - Volume I: Setting the Stage*, this was one of the few barometers that could be used to measure the success of the campaigns.[1]

President Trump entertained over 1.1 million people at his rallies leading up to the election. On the other hand, Joe Biden saw a total of less than 2,000 people at his rallies. The upcoming 2020 Election looked like it would be a landslide for President Trump based on these numbers.[2]

In *The Steal - Volume II: The Impossible Occurs,* more information was provided on these numbers. A month before the 2020 Election, both President Trump and Biden held campaign events. President Trump was in cold Duluth, Minnesota, where an estimated ten thousand people attended his rally. Joe Biden held an event in Phoenix with only a couple of handfuls of attendees. But the disparity was just as large online. President Trump had about 2.5 million

1 (Hoft J., FINAL 2020 RALLY TALLY: President Trump Had Largest Crowds at His Rallies in US History—Biden Had Some of the Smallest, 2020).

2 Ibid

viewers of his rally in Duluth when adding up online views across media platforms. Joe Biden had a combined 75,000 viewers of his Arizona event. No one was following Biden. Biden received only three percent of the viewership that President Trump received.[3]

Early in the morning of November 4, 2020, at around 3:00 a.m., Americans finally went to bed. It appeared that President Trump had the 2020 Election in the bag. President Trump was up big in Wisconsin, Michigan, Pennsylvania, and Georgia. These states would give him the win.

Nevada, North Carolina, and Arizona were not finished counting—their results which could go either way—but President Trump had the overall lead based on these late-night results, and it looked like the win was his. However, for some reason, the media would not call the race for President Trump. Big Tech giants had warned us a month before the election that we would not know the winner of the Presidential Election on election night. This bizarre warning was coming to fruition.

In the early morning of November 4, 2020, hundreds of thousands of votes were added to Joe Biden's totals in Wisconsin and Michigan. Just enough votes were added to these states' totals to give Biden the win. As discussed in *The Steal - Volume II: The Impossible Occurs*, over the next three days after the election, hundreds of thousands of votes were added to Joe Biden's totals in Pennsylvania and Georgia, giving him the lead in these two states as well.

THE IMPOSSIBLE OCCURRED.

The Mainstream media or Big Media immediately joined the chorus of pundits who made claims that the election was perfect. Everything was fine. For an industry that lost so much integrity during the past decade and especially after candidate and then-President Trump won the Presidency, Big Media's efforts to ignore the thousands of instances of fraud and corruption in the 2020 Election were the worst. The little credibility that Big Media had left was gone.

---

3 Hoft J., OMG! NO ONE Is Showing Up to Biden-Harris Events and NO ONE Is Watching Online—Biden-Harris Have Only 3% of President Trump's Online Viewership, 2020.

The tens of millions of Trump voters who voted for him in record-setting numbers wanted to know what happened, but Big Media wouldn't tell them. The once great conservative media outlet *FOX News* lost much of its audience on election night with its reporting and with its lack of reporting of the election steal after the election.

As time went on, Americans demanded investigations and audits. These efforts were stalled by numerous individuals, sidelined by lawfare, and disrupted by bad actors. The activities after the 2020 Election to sideline the audits and investigations into the election were thought through, coordinated, and planned.

Bad actors were inserted into efforts to cover up the 2020 election crimes, and likely a lot of money was made by these bad actors for their efforts to sideline and sidetrack the real efforts to undress the stolen election.

Watching all this, the candid observer could see the magnitude of the effort to steal the election from President Trump and the American people. With hindsight looking back at the trillions of dollars at stake and the impact on all the countries around the world, it should have come as no surprise that the bad actors would do anything to ensure the 2020 Election was stolen from President Trump.

Bad actors and foreign nations would all be happy to see the US run by radicals with the sole purpose of destroying this great country. They weren't going to allow anyone to uncover the election steal.

Wikipedia defines a cover-up as follows:[4]

> A **cover-up** is an attempt, whether successful or not, to conceal evidence of wrongdoing, error, incompetence, or other embarrassing information. Research has distinguished personal cover-ups (covering up one's own misdeeds) from relational cover-ups (covering up someone else's misdeeds).
>
> The expression is usually applied to people in positions of authority who abuse power to avoid or silence criticism or to deflect guilt of

---

4 (Wikipedia, 2023)

wrongdoing. Perpetrators of a cover-up (initiators or their allies) may be responsible for a misdeed, a breach of trust or duty, or a crime.

The 2020 Election was stolen. Declaring Joe Biden "the winner" was laughable. It was impossible. The way the election was stolen is well covered in the second volume in this series – *The Steal - Volume II: The Impossible Occurs.* The numerous efforts to cover up this steal are described in the following chapters.

President Trump received a record number of votes. Joe Biden didn't come close to legitimately winning. A massive cover-up ensued to ensure that the 2020 Election "win" for Joe Biden was not overturned.

2

Zero Enforcement

Americans woke up on November 4, 2020, to see that the results of the 2020 election had changed. Many Americans stayed up to see the winner declared on election night, as had occurred in all modern elections prior to this. But 2020 was different.

The media's reporting was very suspicious. Many American voters followed *FOX News* on election night. In 2016, President Trump was ahead from start to finish. Kentucky and Indiana were called first, and Trump won them. After that, he won enough states to stay in the lead the entire night. But this didn't happen in 2020. Not because he didn't win many of the same states as he did in 2020, but because there appeared to be a concerted effort on the part of the media to never place President Trump in the lead.

Florida and Texas, both states President Trump won in 2016, did very well for him in 2020, but these states were never called when it appeared certain that President Trump had won them. This allowed Joe Biden's camp to hold the lead throughout the night. Then at around 3:00 a.m. EST, President Trump gave a quick speech noting that his campaign was way ahead in Wisconsin, Michigan, Pennsylvania, and Georgia. Yet, for some reason, the media would not call them for Trump.

At 6:00 a.m. EST, when these same Americans woke up, Wisconsin and Michigan had flipped to the Biden camp. We soon learned that there were huge drops of ballots for Biden that put Biden in the lead in Wisconsin and Michigan. A few days later, both Pennsylvania and Georgia were awarded to Biden, putting him ahead for good. The details behind these numbers and what happened were covered extensively in *The Steal - Volume II: The Impossible Occurs.*

As noted in that book (*Volume II*), the man behind the infamous Dilbert cartoon, Scott Adams, provided his observations in a short video that was shared on Twitter by Dr. Kelly Ward, the chair of the Arizona Republican Party, in early December 2020. Adams said the following while sharing this viral video:[5]

> Everybody is looking for this little bit of evidence of whether the election was stolen or not. It's complete misdirection. **You don't need evidence if bullies chased out the witnesses**. Let me say that again. Bullies chased out witnesses in the key cities. So, keep that fact, that one little fact. Bullies chased out witnesses to the vote count. [Next, the video shows individuals being bullied and stopped from observing the election ballot counting process in various locations.]
>
> **Every f——king thing you say after that doesn't matter. All that matters is that it was non-transparent by force.** And if you allow yourself to imagine that other stuff matters, you're a victim of misinformation and misdirection.

As soon as Americans were bullied and stopped from observing what was really going on in the election, the election was over. Everything needed to stop. Law enforcement should have stepped in and arrested the bullies who were committing election crimes. The results in the areas where the counting lacked oversight should have been thrown out and done over.

> ***Where was law enforcement? Our elections were being stolen, and law enforcement looked the other way.***

5 (Ward, 2020)

Americans witnessed crimes occurring. The same actions were occurring across the country but specifically in major cities in swing states.

PHILADELPHIA

As in prior years, Philadelphia was again a major problem in the 2020 Election. In fact, it was worse than it has ever been. On the Thursday, two days after the election, President Trump's former Campaign Manager, Corey Lewandowski, shared the following from the City of Brotherly Love:[6]

> Here's where we are. Every second they're counting additional ballots with NO OBSERVERS in the city of Philadelphia. They're not telling us when they're going to finish counting in Philadelphia … We've had a court order in place effective since 9:30 this morning. They dismissed it. There is no enforcement mechanism. We asked the sheriff to come and enforce it. He patently said no. We asked the election office to enforce it. They said no. And you know if they can do this to the President of the United States, what is the next court they don't have to listen to?
>
> *(This was prophetic, as you'll see in subsequent chapters.)*

There was no law enforcement to be found. Americans were prevented from seeing what was going on in the Philadelphia Convention Center after the election, despite a court order obtained after the election requiring these observers be allowed into the facility. Americans weren't allowed to see what was happening and no one in Philadelphia seemed to care.

Over the three days after the election, Joe Biden was awarded the win in Pennsylvania after making up more than 700,000 votes to overcome his deficit on election day. This all happened while Americans were prevented from seeing what was going on.

---

6 (Hoft J. , Corey Lewandowski: Philly Law Enforcement told Us They WILL NOT Enforce Court Order that Demands Election Observers (VIDEO), 2020)

DETROIT

In Detroit, there were similar actions but a different response from law enforcement. Michigan resident and founder of the website *100 Percent Fed Up*, Patty McMurray, arrived in Detroit the morning of November 4 planning on being a poll watcher. But her plans quickly turned into a nightmare.[7]

Patty shared that despite there being COVID protocols in place, there were extra people at every table in the huge facility who weren't poll watchers or workers. It appeared that these individuals' jobs were to harass Republican poll watchers. The GOP poll watchers had large name plates placed on their clothing so they could be easily identified like Jews in Nazi Germany.[8]

When a GOP poll watcher eventually had enough and spoke out, the police would intervene. Instead of dealing with the individuals harassing GOP poll watchers, the police would escort the GOP poll watcher out of the room. Each time this happened, the room would roar with applause.[9]

At some point during the day, the military votes were scheduled to come out. Patty and others took a quick break, knowing these votes were coming, but when they arrived back to this monstrous room, they were locked out. Patty shared:[10]

> Half of our GOP workers were locked outside and couldn't come in. So, they started the military vote with only about 40 of us inside and there were 134 tables. They knew that we couldn't oversee the ballots and that's why they were locking us out. It had nothing to do with there was too many people in the room. They called the health inspector down to say there were too many people in the room. Well, if there were too many people in the room, maybe some of the Democrat agitators who didn't have any credentials should have left the room?

---

7 (Hoft J. , EXCLUSIVE: Detroit Ballot Counters Were Counting "Xerox Copies" as Actual Military Votes (Video), 2020)

8 Ibid

9 Ibid

10 Ibid

> Those people didn't leave the room. There were two to three of those people at almost every table when I got there.
>
> So they locked the GOP workers out so we couldn't watch over the military ballots. Once we started counting the military ballots, I realized why they locked us out.
>
> They started opening the ballots, and the ballots are in regular envelopes, right. They are addressed to the Detroit City Clerk from overseas, many of them. And so, they would open the ballots, and in almost every case, it was a Xerox copy of a ballot, and the ballots looked very similar every time they opened them, which is really strange to me, because another thing that's really strange to me: every single ballot without exception at the table where I was working from, the military was a non-registered voter, and without exception, they voted for a straight Democrat or at least for ... Joe Biden and Gary Peters. Both who happen to be the worst candidates in the world.
>
> I mean, seriously, nobody votes for Joe Biden unless they hate Trump so bad that it's just a vote against Trump. But nobody votes for Gary Peters, Senator Gary Peters, because nobody knows who Senator Gary Peters is.

In Detroit, it wasn't that law enforcement didn't show up, it was that law enforcement facilitated the election steal. To this day, no one has addressed the many crimes poll watchers in Michigan saw and experienced the day after the 2020 Election.

Late Night White Van

President Trump was ahead of Joe Biden in the swing state of Michigan by over 100,000 votes on election day. This appeared to be another solid win for President Trump in Michigan with a greater margin of victory than in 2016.[11]

11 (Hoft J. , Dirtbag Bill Barr Said Driving Vanloads of Ballots into Detroit's TCF Center Late at Night was "Entirely Normal" – Blocking GOP Observers from Counting Room Was Acceptable, 2021)

But then, at the TCF Center in Detroit, formerly known as Cobo Hall, in the middle of the night, vehicles were spotted delivering ballots to the TCF Center early in the morning on November 4. At least three election observers testified in sworn affidavits that they witnessed this event.[12]

The ballot drop at 3:30 a.m. was the first load of ballots received at the Center since 10:30 p.m. on Election night. This was significant because later at 6:30 a.m., 141,000 ballots were recorded in the election, with 96 percent of these ballots going to Joe Biden.[13]

US Attorney General Bill Barr was not interested in this event. He reportedly told President Trump this was "entirely normal" and acceptable practice to receive a large number of ballots early in the morning under the TCF Center from suspicious characters driving a white van. Barr also disregarded the hundreds of signed affidavits from election observers who observed fraud at the TCF Center or were prevented from performing their duties as observers. Barr also completely ignored the fact the GOP observers were banished and blocked from entering the ballot counting room in Detroit later that day.[14]

A Truckload of Ballots from New York to Pennsylvania

In Pennsylvania, a different event was being investigated after the 2020 Election. Lt Col Tony Shaffer (retired) is the President of the London Center for Policy Research, a New York Times bestselling author, and CIA trained intelligence operations officer with 35 years of experience in global and national security. After the 2020 Election, Shaffer was one of many Americans who offered to help investigate the results of the 2020 Election.[15]

---

12 Ibid

13 Ibid

14 Ibid

15 (Hoft J. , AG Barr Told Lt. Col. Tony Shaffer to Stop Looking Into Truck Driver Jesse Morgan's Testimony That He Moved More Than 200,000 Fraudulent Ballots from NY to PA Before the 2020 Election, 2021)

Shaffer was in Pennsylvania after the election when a tip came in from a truck driver who drove a route for the US Postal Service. Jesse Morgan came out after the election and claimed that he picked up a load of ballots in envelopes in October 2020 and delivered this trailer load from New York to Pennsylvania. After many corrupt acts were identified in the conservative media after the election, Morgan decided to share his story. Shaffer was there to listen to and vet Morgan and his story.[16]

After a period of time and much research and validation of Morgan and his story, Shaffer was convinced that Morgan was telling the truth - that a very suspicious truckload of completed ballots was delivered from New York to Pennsylvania before the election.[17]

Shaffer called his old friend and former US Attorney General under President Reagan, Ed Meese, with the story. Meese contacted AG Bill Barr and filled him in on what Shaffer had shared with him. Within ten minutes, Shaffer received a call from Barr. Shaffer later described this conversation:[18]

> Not 10 minutes go by, Joe, and all the sudden, I get a call from a 202 number. "Hey Tony, this is Bill Barr. What's going on?"
>
> And I go through and explain what we just talked about. And he says, "You need to stop. You are interfering with my investigation." (What?)
>
> "Where is Mr. Morgan now?" And I told him we had him in a safe house . . . "You will stop now. You will turn him over to us immediately. You are now interfering in an FBI investigation."
>
> I said and I explained to him that with all due respect, the FBI is not the organization to be investigating this based on all the problems.
>
> "No, they're the ones that are working this. You have no authority to continue doing anything that you are doing!"

---

16 Ibid

17 Ibid

18 (Hoft J. , "Bill Barr Broke the Law… The Fix Is In… Bill Barr Did Not Do His Job" – EXCLUSIVE VIDEO: Tony Shaffer on Barr's Actions After the 2020 Election, 2022)

> And basically for the next 20 minutes, he yelled at me on the phone.

Shaffer went on to say that he wanted to give Morgan whistleblower status, but Barr wouldn't have it.[19]

For his courage in coming out with his story, Morgan was attacked by the FBI at his house and accused of making the whole thing up. The FBI even asked him who was paying him to make up the story.[20]

Despite piles of affidavits across the country and numerous criminal or suspicious acts seemingly everywhere, AG Bill Barr assured Americans that there just wasn't widespread voter fraud in the 2020 Election. He repeated this claim multiple times after the election. But did he really look?[21]

A former Trump adviser, Jeffrey Clark, the Director of Litigation at the Center for Renewing America, joined Steve Bannon on his War Room in September of 2022, nearly two years after the 2020 Election. Clark told Bannon that the Center for Renewing America sent out FOIA requests to 12 US Attorney districts located in the 2020 battleground states.[22]

Clark told Steve Bannon that the FOIA requests came back from every district but one with no documents. No investigations were carried out. At that point in time, only one of the 12 districts had not yet replied, and that's the Eastern District of Pennsylvania. The US Attorney of the Eastern District asked to investigate issues in his district, but Barr famously denied the request![23]

After the election of 2020, America learned that Attorney General Bill Barr was not who they thought he was. He ignored the many illegal acts identified after the election that should have been addressed. Individuals were committing crimes, and nothing was being done.

---

19 Ibid

20 Op cit, AG Barr Told...

21 (Hoft J. , BARR LIED! FOIA Requests Reveal There Were No DOJ Investigations on Election Fraud After 2020 Election as Bill Barr Claims (VIDEO), 2022)

22 Ibid

23 Ibid

It was clear that law enforcement across the nation had been told to stand down. No one was coming to the rescue. An election was being stolen in broad daylight, and the burglars were allowed to commit their crimes as if no one cared.

Due to these election crimes, many believed that the election should not be certified until there was confidence in the results. A different strategy was needed to address the many perceived crimes that occurred across numerous states.

3

EVIDENCE IGNORED

THIS CHAPTER INCLUDES several issues and items raised in front of legislatures across the country after the 2020 Election. To see more information on the 2020 Election not included below, please read The Steal - Volume II: The Impossible Occurs.

After it was clear that the election was stolen and law enforcement wasn't going to help address the many crimes identified in the 2020 Presidential Election, President Trump and his team decided to bring the crimes and unlawful acts identified in the election to the state legislatures in key states. The state legislatures had the final say on elections per the US Constitution.

President Trump picked his good friend and attorney, Rudy Giuliani, to lead this effort. Immediately, the corrupt Big Media attempted to smear President Trump, Rudy, and his team.

On November 24, 2020, three weeks after Election Day, the Trump team announced that they were going to hold presentations over the upcoming week in front of Pennsylvania, Arizona, and Michigan legislatures, all of which were led by Republicans. Initially, this sounded pretty good, with President Trump's team wanting to provide confidence that all legal votes were counted, and all illegal votes were not counted in the November 3rd election.[24]

---

24 (Hoft J. , Pennsylvania, Michigan and Arizona Announce Election Fraud Hearings, 2020)

The President's attorney, Rudy Giuliani, and his team would present before these legislatures the many reasons that the results in the 2020 Presidential election should not be certified. It was a tall order, but something needed to be done to protect the union and save the country from an invalid result in the 2020 Presidential Election.

Pennsylvania

The first presentation occurred on Wednesday, November 25, in front of the Pennsylvania Senate in Gettysburg, Pennsylvania. Giuliani and team spent hours at this historic location providing ample evidence that the 2020 Election results in Pennsylvania were invalid.

One witness described how he personally observed dozens of USB cards being uploaded to voting machines in a short period of time, which resulted in 50,000 votes for Joe Biden. Another witness described huge "spikes" in Pennsylvania ballots that went 600,000 to Joe Biden and 3,200 to Trump, and the crowd gasped.[25]

Rudy Giuliani pointed two huge gaps with Pennsylvania's mail-in ballots:[26]

> "You have two major gaps—you have the 672,770 votes that were not inspected by anyone secretly put into the ballot box, and then you have this gap that I don't understand between the mail-in ballots. You've sent out: 1.8 million, and the number you counted: 2.5 million!" Rudy said.
>
> Rudy continued, "That's totally impossible to explain other than what some of the other witnesses were suggesting, that they were basically stuffing the ballot box. I believe what happened was that they never expected to be behind by 700,000 or 800,000 votes on election night. They expected to be behind by a couple hundred thousand in Philadelphia to steal a couple hundred thousand votes. They do it every

25 (Laila, Giuliani Points Out Major Problem with Mail-In Ballots in Pennsylvania: Only 1.8 Mail-In Ballots Were Sent Out – But 2.5 Million Were Counted (VIDEO), 2020)

26 Ibid

> year. That's not going to be tough. Now you have a real big problem, so you had to create mail-in ballots, you had to stretch it out for a while . . ."

During the presentation in Gettysburg, President Trump called in, and the participants and observers at the hearing began cheering, "Trump, Trump, Trump." The President shared with everyone there, especially Rudy:[27]

> We have all the evidence. We have all the affidavits. We have everything. All we need is to have some judge listen to it properly without having a political opinion or another kind of problem. By the way, the evidence is pouring in now as we speak. And by the way, I want to thank Rudy Giuliani for having the courage to do this. (applause) . . . Rudy you were the greatest mayor in New York. You saw what happened to New York without Rudy. But this is more important, what you are doing now. This is far more important than being a great mayor from the City of New York and being its greatest mayor by far. This is going to be your crowning achievement. (applause)

There was no vote that day in Pennsylvania. The evidence was clear. The election could not be certified due to the hundreds of thousands of ballot issues. But nothing was done. The day before Rudy arrived the corrupt Democrat Secretary of State, Kathy Boockvar, and corrupt Democrat Governor, Tom Wolf, certified the results of the 2020 Election for Joe Biden.[28]

ARIZONA

On Monday, November 30, 2020, Rudy and his team arrived in Phoenix, Arizona, to discuss the results of the 2020 election in Arizona. Like in

---

27 (Hoft J. , "This is Going to Be Your Crowning Achievement!" – Pennsylvania Crowd APPLAUDS President Trump and Rudy Giuliani — Start Chanting, "Trump! Trump! Trump!..." at Gettysburg Hearing (VIDEO), 2020)

28 (Laila, JUST IN: Pennsylvania Secretary of State Certifies Election Results, 2020)

Gettysburg the week before, piles of affidavits were presented, and numerous individuals spoke in front of the Arizona Senate.

Rudy Giuliani opened the meeting, and the crowd erupted in cheers as Rudy Giuliani issued a clarion call to state lawmakers: "I'm gonna ask you to fight . . . Your political career is worth losing if you can save the right to vote in America."[29]

Dr. Shiva Ayyadurai presented and showed that per his analysis of the results in Arizona, the only way for Joe Biden to have statistically caught up with President Trump was if Democrat votes came in at 130% for Biden and -30% for Trump. This was impossible.[30]

One witness testified that the signatures on the ballots that were coming in "didn't even resemble" what they were matching to on file. In addition, the same witness also said that truckloads of ballots kept coming in for ten days after elections officials thought they were done counting votes.[31]

"Ten days before they quit tabulating . . . They thought they were done [counting ballots], and then more truckloads of ballots were coming in. I'm like, 'how can you not know how many ballots are still out there?'"[32]

In the middle of the hearing, Arizona's corrupt Democrat Secretary of State, Katie Hobbs, certified the results in Arizona, giving Joe Biden the state by 10,000 votes. The corrupt GOP governor, Doug Ducey, then certified the results as well. President Trump called in and blasted Ducey, and the crowd booed. Despite piles of evidence showing the 2020 Election never should have been certified in Arizona, the corrupt Governor and Secretary of State certified the results on that day.[33]

---

29 (Laila, Dr. Shiva Presents Data at Arizona Hearing That Completely Obliterates Biden Victory Narrative (VIDEO), 2020)

30 Ibid

31 (Laila, Arizona Witness: Truck Loads of Ballots Kept Coming in For 10 Days After Elections Officials Thought They Were Done Counting Votes (VIDEO), 2020)

32 Ibid

33 (Laila, President Trump Calls Into Hearing on Voting Irregularities in Arizona, Blasts RINO Gov. Doug Ducey (VIDEO), 2020)

MICHIGAN

The next day on Tuesday, December 1, 2020, Rudy Giuliani and his team landed in Michigan to discuss the 2020 Election results there. It was amazing seeing all that had been put together in such a short period of time for these three meetings in front of the legislatures in Pennsylvania, Arizona, and Michigan. Like the prior two presentations, Rudy came prepared with piles of affidavits as well as expert testimonies, providing an ample amount of evidence that the election should never have been certified for Joe Biden.

Much of the same information that was presented to concerned politicians in Pennsylvania and Arizona was included in Rudy's presentation in Detroit, only this time, it focused on Michigan. During the presentations to the members of the Michigan legislature, the challenging thing for the observer was to figure out who were the Democrat politicians and who were the Republicans. This was because the Republicans in Michigan had the same attitude towards Rudy as the Democrats did. It was hard to watch at times and no doubt challenging for Rudy and his team to handle, but they courageously moved ahead and shared the truth.

Numerous individuals shared their stories in Michigan, like those who shared in Pennsylvania and Arizona. One individual in Michigan who presented was a beautiful young lady by the name of Melissa Carone. Carone was hired by Dominion for the 2020 Election in Michigan. During her presentation in response to a question from a Democrat concerning her integrity, Carone responded: "I signed an affidavit under penalty of prison . . . Did you?"[34]

Carone then went on to ask why more witnesses hadn't stepped forward. That's when she went off: "I'll tell you why. My life has been destroyed. My life has been completely destroyed because of this! . . . I can't even get a job anymore because **Democrats like to ruin your life**."[35]

On the Sunday after the Michigan presentation, Rudy Giuliani was on with Maria Bartiromo on Sunday Morning Futures, and he shared that he had over 1,000 affidavits to date from people who were willing to testify on the

---

34 (Hoft J. , "I Can't Get a Job Any More Because Democrats Like to Ruin Your Life!" – GOP Witness GOES OFF at Michigan Hearing (VIDEO), 2020)

35 Ibid

irregularities and potential crimes they observed during the 2020 Election. These signed affidavits were from election officials and observers both Republican and Democrat willing to speak out on the massive voter fraud in the election.[36]

Rudy's time and effort to put together the presentation in Michigan were ignored. The state went on to certify the fraudulent results for Joe Biden. Despite piles of evidence and affidavits the GOP controlled legislature couldn't be bothered.

GEORGIA

Rudy Giuliani and his team visited Georgia on December 3, 2020, and presented in front of the Georgia Senate Judiciary Subcommittee on Elections and members of the Senate Judiciary Committee. Giuliani urged the state lawmakers to act. The election was certified by the corrupt Georgia Secretary of State and Governor, who were both Republicans.[37]

There were many topics discussed and issues presented in front of the Senate Subcommittee that day. The committee, led by Chairperson William T. Ligon, a former judge, went on to issue a report from its review of issues in Georgia.[38]

The beginning of Ligon's report states that **"any reported results [from the 2020 Election] must be viewed as untrustworthy."**

The report went on to describe the 2020 Election activities in Georgia per testimonies and affidavits provided to the committee. There was a lack of enforcement of the law and sloppy handling of ballots by those counting. A

---

36 (Hoft J. , "The FBI Is Nowhere to be Found!" – Rudy Giuliani Reveals UNDENIABLE VOTER FRAUD in 2020 Election – Now Has 1,000 Signed Witness Affidavits! (VIDEO), 2020)

37 (Laila, "This Stops Right Now!" – Rudy Giuliani Testifies on Election Fraud, Urges Georgia Lawmakers to Take Action #StopTheSteal (VIDEO), 2020)

38 (Hoft J. , ARROGANT CORRUPTION: To This Day Georgia's Secretary of State Raffensperger IGNORES Multiple Issues Identified by President Trump's Auditor and Georgia State Senator and former Judge William Ligon from the 2020 Election, 2022)

great deal of evidence supported a coordinated effort to prevent a transparent process of observing the counting of ballots during the absentee ballot opening period and on Election Night.[39]

The report went on to describe numerous events from multiple individuals that occurred during the 2020 election. One individual by the name of Scott Hall testified that he was told to leave the World Congress Center in Fulton County after he tried to document and photograph nine unsecured bags of ballots. He testified that he "cried" over the incidents that he saw.[40]

Rudy Giuliani's team presented for five hours on December 3 in front of the Georgia Senate Judiciary Subcommittee on Elections and members of the Senate Judiciary Committee. A month later, a report was drafted by President Trump's auditor and provided to Georgia Secretary of State Brad Raffensperger, who ignored both this report and Senator Ligon's report. Nothing was done about the corrupt Georgia results in response to this work and these reports.[41]

Christina Bobb, in her book *Stealing Your Vote* about the 2020 Election, says:[42]

Just like in Arizona, Wisconsin, Pennsylvania and Michigan, Georgia Republicans proved to be the biggest obstacle in election transparency.

In June 2021, far-left CNN reported that Georgia investigators were looking into Rudy's presentation in early December to determine how they could charge Giuliani for fighting for free and fair elections. *CNN* reported:[43]

> Georgia investigators are scrutinizing Rudy Giuliani's appearance before state lawmakers in 2020, where he peddled baseless claims of voter fraud and encouraged legislators to appoint a new slate of presidential electors.
>
> The special purpose grand jury—which has been investigating whether former President Donald Trump or his allies violated the law

39 Ibid

40 Ibid

41 Ibid

42 (Bobb, 2023)

43 (Murray, 2021)

> in their efforts to flip the 2020 election results in Georgia—has heard testimony from at least four witnesses regarding Giuliani's activities. Three of those witnesses were Georgia Democratic lawmakers, who testified this week, and were at the state Capitol when Giuliani and other Trump lawyers shared conspiracy theory-laden claims of voter fraud in December 2020.

CNN's report never mentions that a report from the presentation in early December 2020 was published by Senator Ligon, who happens to also have been an attorney and judge. The 15-pages of issues were ignored as well as the Executive Summary. This is how the media addressed efforts to have the tens of thousands of election issues unearthed after the election.

While Rudy was trying to encourage state legislatures to address the many issues identified after the 2020 Elections, legal challenges were taking place in the courts. Americans wanted justice and Rudy Giuliani and his team were doing their best to address the election steal using every legal remedy possible. Unfortunately, these efforts often fell on deaf ears.

4

THE COURTS

BEFORE THE 2020 Election, the Democrats used the courts in a systematic way to ensure that they could steal the election. As noted in *The Steal - Volume I: Setting the Stage*:[44]

> The problem for the Democrats was that any changes in voting processes were to be addressed by the legislatures per the state constitutions, and there wasn't enough time to make these changes. The Democrats had to amend state election processes without the legally required vote in the state legislatures. So, they went to work.
>
> Hillary Clinton's attorney from her 2016 campaign was Marc Elias. He was an attorney at Perkins Coie specializing in political law. He became the lead attorney in multiple actions around the country in 2020 to ensure absentee ballots were easily distributed in the 2020 Election.

Elias focused his efforts on some key swing states. He was in Wisconsin, and somehow he managed to acquire the signatures of Secretary of State Robin Vos and Senate Majority Leader Scott Fitzgerald (both Republicans). Vos is a good

44 (Hoft J. , The Steal - Volume I: Setting the Stage, 2022)

friend of former House Speaker Paul Ryan who hates President Trump. These GOP leaders signed agreements with Elias implementing ballot drop boxes in the state.[45]

After refusing to hear a case on drop boxes immediately after the 2020 Election, the Wisconsin Supreme Court finally heard a case on these election boxes in early July 2022. Nearly two years after the 2020 Election, the court ruled that drop boxes were illegal in the state. The Wisconsin election results in 2020 never should have been certified and certainly not for Joe Biden.[46]

Elias didn't stop in Wisconsin. In Georgia, Elias cut two deals with Republican Secretary of State Brad Raffensperger. These deals altered the state's absentee ballot procedures. Many don't believe that Raffensperger had the right to sign these agreements.[47]

Elias was also active in Pennsylvania. One agreement allowed the state to receive ballots up to three days after the election. This went all the way to the US Supreme Court before the election. It was allowed to stand after newly-appointed Justice Amy Coney Barrett refused to opine on the case.[48]

After the election, a case was brought forward claiming the change in the law for absentee ballots that took place in 2019 was unconstitutional. Marc Elias represented the Democrats in this case, and it was quickly thrown out by the far-left Pennsylvania Supreme Court.[49]

The Democrats knew that they needed mail-in ballots to steal the election. They changed laws in states to make this happen using COVID-19 as the rationale for doing so.

This was only the beginning of the lawfare to take place in the 2020 election. As the results started rolling in on election night, it soon became clear that something was amiss. The morning after the election, it was clear that material election-changing wrongdoing had occurred.

---

45 Ibid

46 (Hoft J. , BREAKING BIG: Wisconsin Supreme Court Rules Public Absentee Drop Boxes ILLEGAL!, 2022)

47 Op cit, Volume I

48 Ibid

49 Ibid

President Trump and the American people who voted for him in the tens of millions wanted the law enforced and their votes protected. The courts were going to have to right the wrongs by the Democrats and Trump haters who manufactured a Joe Biden win.

THE DREAM TEAM

The President put together a legal team that included some of the best lawyers today, if not in US history. Online, this team was referred to as the "Dream Team." With this group of seasoned and successful attorneys, it looked like President Trump had a chance.[50]

Rudy Giuliani led the list. The former DOJ prosecutor in New York who took on the mob was one of the best attorneys alive to represent the President's cases across the country. He was elected mayor of New York because of his prosecutorial work, and he turned the city around. He later represented President Trump as his personal attorney.

Attorney Joe diGenova and his wife, Victoria Toensing, showed up in defense of President Trump. DiGenova is the former US Attorney over the District of Columbia and a frequent guest on radio and TV shows across the country. Victoria Toensing often appears with her husband, and both have storied careers as DC lawyers. Although not part of President Trump's legal team, they were involved in communicating with the media about the election.[51]

Jay Sekulow was on the team. This man, who looks like a modern-day Clark Kent, was one of the President's attorneys who represented him and won against the criminals in the DOJ attempting to remove President Trump in the Deep State's coup referred to as the Mueller investigation. Sekulow also represented the President in the bogus impeachment proceedings from the corrupt Democrat House.[52]

---

50 (Hoft J. , President Trump's Dream Team Is the Greatest Assembly of Attorneys in US History Fighting for the Survival of the Nation, 2020)

51 Ibid

52 Ibid

Sekulow is described as follows:[53]

> Jay Sekulow is widely regarded as one of the foremost free speech and religious liberties litigators in the United States, having argued 12 times before the US Supreme Court in some of the most groundbreaking First Amendment cases of the past quarter century. As Chief Counsel of the American Center for Law and Justice (ACLJ), he is a renowned constitutional attorney, an international expert on religious liberty, and an acclaimed and distinguished broadcaster. Jay Sekulow is a passionate advocate for protecting religious and constitutional freedoms with an impressive track record of success. His steadfast determination and commitment to protecting these freedoms is expansive with his work resulting in a lasting impact across America and around the world.

Jenna Ellis was on the team. She was a young and smart attorney who also worked for President Trump in the past. She was a newcomer to the President's team, but she held herself like a seasoned veteran. Ellis is a great public speaker, and she knew that those against the President hated the President and America.[54]

Sidney Powell also helped with legal efforts after the election.[55] Many people learned who she was when she outed the Mueller gang during President Trump's first term. She had a solid career in the DOJ and then represented individuals who were caught up in the Enron scandal in the 2000s. Powell represented at least one individual who was targeted by Robert Mueller and Andrew Weissmann, who were working for the government at that time. Powell learned how corrupt these people were in their attempts to indict innocent Americans.

---

53 (Sekulow, 2023)

54 Op cit, Hoft – Dream Team

55 Ibid

Powell's knowledge of the Deep State and characters like Mueller and Weissmann helped her when she took on General Michael Flynn's case against the government. She uncovered that the Deep State lied. He was innocent, and they pressured him to agree to a bogus plea deal.

Powell uncovered the government's lies, and as a result, the DOJ agreed to drop all charges against General Flynn. President Trump ended up pardoning the General after a corrupt DC judge wouldn't drop the case after all parties agreed to end it. Powell showed her legal knowledge and expertise at this time.

Professor John Eastman from Chapman University was also a member of the team. He was the former Dean of Chapman's School of Law and was affiliated with the Claremont Institute as a Senior Fellow and Director of the Institute's Center for Constitutional Jurisprudence. Prior to joining the Fowler School of Law faculty in August 1999, he served as a law clerk with Justice Clarence Thomas at the Supreme Court of the United States. He was a brilliant attorney well versed in the law.[56]

Other attorneys like Lin Wood joined the fight against the certification of the corrupted election. Wood is famous for representing Richard Jewell, who was wrongly accused of a bombing in Atlanta during the 1996 Olympics. He also has represented a number of individuals wrongfully defamed by the Big Media and others. His communication skills are powerful and persuasive.

This arguably was the greatest team of lawyers put together in US history. Together, their accomplishments included taking on the mob, the crooked DOJ, and Big Media. The team included the successful mayor of New York City who made that city even better after 9/11. This group also included an attorney who had a Mueller case dropped right before sentencing, and so much more. The team was the best, but this wasn't enough.

2020 Election Cases

Numerous cases were filed with the courts related to the results in the 2020 Election. Attorney Sidney Powell was behind some big cases in some of the key

56 (University, 2023)

swing states. It was clear that these states were standing behind the certification of their uncertifiable results for Joe Biden (See *The Steal - Volume II: The Impossible Occurs* for ample evidence why the results in key swing states never should have been certified for Joe Biden).

On November 21, 2020, Attorney Sidney Powell announced on *Newsmax* that she was going to drop some big election cases and she was starting with Georgia. She shared, "Georgia is the first state I'm going to blow up. And Mr. Kemp and the Secretary of State need to go with it, because they're in on this Dominion scam with their last-minute purchase!"[57]

A couple of days later, attorney Lin Wood announced that Powell was going to release her case in Georgia the day before Thanksgiving.[58] Sure enough, Powell filed her case in Georgia on November 25, 2020. Powell said she was releasing the Kraken (a reference to the monster from the movie *Clash of the Titans*).[59]

In an announcement from an attorney connected to General Michael Flynn, Abigail Frye shared in a tweet:[60]

The Kraken came down to Georgia on this Thanksgiving Eve in the form of a 104 pg BOMBSHELL complaint exposing the massive fraud that overwhelmed the 2020 Georgia Elections. Georgia, you are most certainly on our minds. Link to filing to come, stay tuned!

Powell's case included piles of evidence of election fraud in Georgia, including a mention of 96,600 ballots that were requested and counted but were never recorded as being returned to county election boards by the voter. This was a lot of votes considering the election was given to Biden three days after the election by 12,000 votes. The filing was full of evidence like this

57 (Hoft J. , "Georgia Is the First State I'm Going to Blow Up and Mr. Kemp and the Secretary of State Need to Go With It!" — Sidney Powell Releases the Kraken!, 2020)

58 (Hoft J. , HAPPY THANKSGIVING! Lin Wood Announces Sidney Powell Will File Major Lawsuit in Georgia Tomorrow!, 2020)

59 (Hoft J. , BREAKING: KRAKEN RELEASED! Attorney Sidney Powell Files 104 Page BOMBSHELL COMPLAINT of Massive Fraud in Georgia Election – Update: Michigan too, 2020)

60 Ibid

pointing out that the election never should have been certified with tens of thousands of votes in question.[61]

Powell initiated similar actions in Michigan, Arizona, and Wisconsin. Lin Wood and President Trump also initiated actions in Georgia. It looked like the President Trump would get his day in court.

In **Georgia**, Powell's case was placed before George W. Bush-appointed Judge Timothy Batten Sr. On December 7, Judge Batten ruled on the case:[62]

> The ruling in Georgia by Judge Timothy Batten Sr. came less than 90 minutes into a hearing in Atlanta federal court, where Powell had claimed that Trump was the victim of massive ballot fraud related to Georgia's use of Dominion voting machines.
>
> "The relief that the plaintiffs seek this court cannot grant," Batten said.
>
> "They ask the court to order the secretary of state to decertify the election results as if such a mechanism even exists, and I find that it does not."
>
> Batten did not rule on the merits of Powell's claim, which were made on behalf of a slate of would-be Trump electors in the Electoral College.

Also, on December 7, 2020, Obama-appointed Judge Linda V. Parker ruled on Powell's case in **Michigan**. It was already suspicious that this case somehow landed in her court. Judge Parker in her 36-page reply ended by saying the case "lacks standing, proposes a remedy that is far too late to enforce – and critically undermines 'faith in the democratic process'."[63]

Despite mountains of evidence of election fraud in Michigan, including vans showing up in the middle of the night at the TCF Center in Detroit and ballot mules caught dropping ballots in drop boxes across the state on video,

---

61 Ibid

62 (Mangan, 2020)

63 (Hoft J. , Obama Judge in Michigan Labels Sidney Powell's Case of Voting Irregularities "An Amalgamation of Theories, Conjecture, and Speculation", 2020)

law enforcement didn't want to investigate, and judges didn't want to adjudicate. The Obama Judge plain and simple didn't want to review the case. She threw it out.

But Judge Parker wasn't through. In addition to dismissing the case, later in August of 2021, Obama Judge Parker asked to have attorneys Sidney Powell and Lin Wood investigated for possible suspension or disbarment for bringing the case.[64]

In **Arizona**, Sidney Powell's efforts were also blocked by an Obama judge. US District Judge Diane Humetewa, who was praised for being the first Hopi Indian judge, and who claims to be a Republican, was placed in her current position by Barack Obama. She was somehow appointed the judge over Powell's case.

Powell filed a 53-page document showing that the results of the 2020 Election in Arizona should never have been certified. Hundreds of thousands of ballots were identified with material issues. Powell also addressed system issues. This all had to be put together within weeks after the 2020 Election. Arizona was awarded to Joe Biden with a 10,000-vote margin a week after the election.[65]

Powell was given very little time in court to go through her monster filing full of evidence and instead had to argue against the defense's motion to dismiss the case on Tuesday, December 8, 2020, in front of Obama Judge Humetewa.[66] It soon became clear that the judge was not interested in Powell's evidence or arguments.

The next day on December 9, 2020, Obama Judge Humetewa dismissed the case. Somehow, in less than 24 hours, Humetewa put together a 29-page ruling throwing out the case. Ask any attorney, and they will tell you that the ruling had to have been drafted before the hearing on December 9. There simply was no way she could have drafted a 29-page document in a few hours

---

64 (Hoft J. , Corrupt Obama Judge Orders Lin Wood and Sidney Powell Be Punished for Daring to Sue the State for Election Fraud in the 2020 Election, 2021)

65 (Scoop, 2020)

66 (Swoyer, 2020)

after the case was heard. Others might even argue that her ruling was provided to her.

In **Wisconsin**, Powell ran into another Obama judge. Chief US District Judge Pamela Pepper, an appointee of Barack Obama, took Powell to task, showing that she (the judge) had no intention of moving forward with her case.[67]

Later in August, when the corrupt Wisconsin governor, Tony Evers, requested that the judge sanction Powell over the case. Judge Pepper declined because she dismissed the case before delving into its merits.[68]

> A Wisconsin federal judge on Thursday denied a request by the state's governor to sanction conservative lawyer Sidney Powell over one of her lawsuits alleging fraud in the 2020 election, leaving the state to cover its own legal fees in the case.
>
> US District Judge Pamela Pepper in Milwaukee ruled that she no longer had jurisdiction over the case, and that sanctions would not be appropriate because she had quickly dismissed Powell's lawsuit before delving into the merits of her claims.

By the end of the day, on December 10, all four of Sidney Powell's "Kraken" cases in Michigan, Arizona, Wisconsin, and Georgia had been dismissed. Evidence that elections were stolen was plentiful, but the courts didn't want to hear it.[69]

Big Media had a field day with the news. They never reported that three of the judges in these cases were Obama judges. Big Media never asked how it could be that three of the most important cases in history landed in front of biased political Obama judges.

Instead, the media crushed attorney Powell mercilessly. In Arizona, a local media outlet shared:[70]

---

67 (Thomsen, 2021)

68 Ibid

69 (Vlamis, 2020)

70 (Week, 2020)

> Powell has claimed to have a wide array of experts and witnesses available to vouch for the alleged fraud in her lawsuits, but Humetewa said she didn't come close to presenting them . . . "This cavalier approach to establishing that hundreds of thousands of Arizona votes were somehow cast in error is itself troublesome," Humetewa said.

What the media didn't say is that Powell was given little to no time to present her many issues, and according to experts reviewing the case, the Obama judge likely had already prepared her dismissal before the hearing and it may have been provided to her.

The Texas Case

Numerous cases popped up after the 2020 Election, but the biggest case of all was the Texas case. On Monday night, December 7, 2020, one month after the 2020 Election, the state of Texas filed a suit against the states of Pennsylvania, Georgia, Michigan and Wisconsin. Texas filed the case with the US Supreme Court, challenging these states' unlawful election procedures.[71]

Texas argued that these four states violated the US Constitution because they made changes to voting rules and procedures through the courts or through executive actions. But these states did not make the changes through the state legislatures as spelled out in the US Constitution. The lawsuit read:

> As set forth in the accompanying brief and complaint, the 2020 election suffered from significant and unconstitutional irregularities in the Defendant States:
>
> • Non-legislative actors' purported amendments to States' duly enacted election laws, in violation of the Electors Clause's vesting

71 (Hoft J. , Texas Files Lawsuit with Supreme Court Challenging Election Procedures in Georgia, Michigan, Pennsylvania and Wisconsin, 2020)

State legislatures with plenary authority regarding the appointment of presidential electors
- Intrastate differences in the treatment of voters, with more favorable allotted to voters – whether lawful or unlawful – in areas administered by local government under Democrat control and with populations with higher ratios of Democrat voters than other areas of Defendant States.
- The appearance of voting irregularities in the Defendant States that would be consistent with the unconstitutional relaxation of ballot-integrity protections in those States' election laws.

One section of the case included some staggering analysis from an expert who studied the election results:[72]

> In the brief submitted to the Supreme Court, Texas includes a declaration from Pacific Economics Group member and USC economics professor, Charles J. Cicchetti, PhD.
>
> Dr. Cicchetti is the former Deputy Director at the Energy and Environmental Policy Center at Harvard University's John Kennedy School of Government and received his PhD in economics from Rutgers University.
>
> According to Dr. Cicchetti, his calculations show the probability of Joe Biden winning the popular vote in the four states independently given President Trump's early lead in those States as of 3:00 a.m. on November 4, 2020, is less than one in a quadrillion.
>
> Dr. Cicchetti's analysis calculates that for Joe Biden to win all four states collectively, the odds of that event happening decrease to less than one in a quadrillion to the fourth power (1 in $1,000,000,000,000,000^4$; i.e., 60 zeros after the one—basically impossible).

72 (Hoft J. , Statistician in Texas Lawsuit Against Georgia, Michigan, Pennsylvania and Wisconsin Says Probability of Biden Winning Election Was One in a Quadrillion!, 2020)

Within two days, 18 states had joined Texas in its suit against Pennsylvania, Georgia, Michigan and Wisconsin. Missouri, Alabama, Arkansas, Florida, Nebraska, North Dakota, Oklahoma, Indiana, Kansas, Louisiana, Mississippi, Montana, South Carolina, South Dakota, Tennessee, Utah, West Virginia, and Arizona joined Texas in its case.[73]

A day later on December 10, 2020, President Trump filed a brief to join the Texas case. Trump, acting "in his personal capacity" as a presidential candidate, sought to intervene in order "to protect his unique and substantial personal interests as a candidate for re-election," his filing stated.[74]

Also on December 10, 106 US House members joined the Texas case against Pennsylvania, Georgia, Michigan, and Wisconsin. These House Republicans signed an amicus brief backing Texas's Supreme Court lawsuit.[75]

On December 11, Minority House Leader Kevin McCarthy joined another group of Republican House Representatives in the House's amicus brief, making it 126 GOP Representatives joining the case.[76] And on the same day, Alaska joined the case, making it 19 states joining Texas in its filing with the Supreme Court.[77]

Rush Limbaugh, only two months before his death, on December 11, shared about how important the Texas case was:[78]

---

73 (Hoft J. , UPDATE: 18 States Join Texas in Supreme Court Lawsuit Against Michigan, Georgia, Wisconsin and Pennsylvania Over Fraudulent Election, 2020)

74 (Laila, President Trump Files Motion to Join Texas Supreme Court Lawsuit Against Pennsylvania, Michigan, Wisconsin and Georgia, 2020)

75 (Laila, 106 House Republicans Sign Brief Backing Texas Supreme Court Lawsuit Against Pennsylvania, Michigan, Georgia and Wisconsin, 2020)

76 (Laila, GOP Minority Leader Kevin McCarthy Joins 125 House Republicans in Supporting Texas Supreme Court Lawsuit Against Pennsylvania, Michigan, Georgia and Wisconsin, 2020)

77. (Hoft J. , https://www.thegatewaypundit.com/2020/12/gop-minority-leader-kevin-mccarthy-joins-125-house-republicans-supporting-texas-supreme-court-lawsuit-pennsylvania-michigan-georgia-wisconsin/, 2020)

78. (Hoft J. , "The US Constitution Is Hanging in the Balance Here" – Rush Limbaugh Lays Out Historic Significance of Texas SCOTUS Lawsuit, 2020)

Again, what this is about boils it down to its essence, these four states changed election law in violation of the way election law is changed, according to the state constitutions of these states. Only the state legislatures can change election law in these states, and the state legislatures have had nothing to do with the changes that took place . . .

. . . **The US Constitution is hanging in the balance here**, because if these four states are allowed to get away with changing something as fundamental as how presidential electors are selected state by state, then the electors in our states are not safe. That's why 17 states have joined Texas here. It's all about the United States Constitution and maintaining it, maintaining its integrity, its primacy.

Now, these other states engaged in this activity because we all know what went on. We all know that they stopped counting at the same time. We all know these states were scared to death what was happening with Trump's lead. They had to stop the count. They had to go find votes. And in the process, they changed election law, and the State of Texas is trying to make sure the Supreme Court understands the gravity of it.

Now, the opponents here say there's nothing to see, this is not a serious violation, the court's not even gonna take this case. That's how weak it is. President Trump has asked to join Texas in the Supreme Court bid to undo the Biden win, although the people will tell you in Texas that's not what they're actually aiming to do. That could be a by-product, but it's not the reason they're doing it.

This is very important to understand. They're not asking the court to pick a winner. They're not asking the court to overturn an election. You see, they think that'll happen if they get a ruling in their favor anyway.

On Friday evening, December 11, 2020, the US Supreme Court dismissed the Texas case claiming a "lack of standing" on the part of Texas.[79]

---

79 (Hoft J. , BREAKING: US Supreme Court Throws Out Texas Lawsuit Against Pennsylvania, Georgia, Michigan and Wisconsin, 2020)

By not reviewing the case, this court set a precedent for the future, allowing one or more states to partake in unconstitutional and even criminal actions that can change the leadership of the legislature or the Presidency, and although greatly affected, there is nothing that any other states can do to address the crimes.

The court refused to see the obvious, that if elections were stolen, nothing else mattered. Elections are the bedrock of our constitutional republic. The court ignored that this is exactly how communists take over countries. All Americans have standing when such grievous election crimes are committed. The Supreme Court failed the US Constitution and the American people.

On December 12, 2020, President Trump tweeted:[80]

> "Justices Alito and Thomas say they would have allowed Texas to proceed with its election lawsuit." @seanhannity This is a great and disgraceful miscarriage of justice. The people of the United States were cheated, and our Country disgraced. Never even given our day in Court!

President Trump was right.

More Election Cases

Attorney Sidney Powell filed four cases with the US Supreme Court on December 11, 2020, for the states of Georgia, Michigan, Arizona, and Wisconsin. These came on the heels of the US Supreme Court decision not to hear the Texas case. Powell shared in a tweet:[81]

> Pay attention! We made emergency filings in #SupremeCourt tonight for #Georgia & #Michigan. Will be filing #Arizona #Wisconsin shortly. These cases raise constitutional issues and prove massive

80 (Hoft J. , These Three Trump Judges Threw the President Under the Bus and the Texas Case in The Garbage, 2020)

81 (Hoft J. , Sidney Powell Announces Emergency Filings in Georgia, Michigan, Arizona and Wisconsin, 2020)

> #fraud. Our plaintiffs have #standing #WeThePeople will not allow #rigged elections Obama judges

The Epoch Times reported on the rationale for Powell's actions in these four states:[82]

> Attorney Sidney Powell is asking the US Supreme Court to immediately intervene in her lawsuits challenging the integrity and outcome of the 2020 elections in four states.
>
> In an announcement on Friday, Powell said she had filed emergency requests to the nation's top court, asking the justices to order officials in Georgia, Michigan, and Arizona to immediately de-certify their 2020 election results and to prevent the states' presidential electors from casting votes in the electoral college.
>
> An emergency filing is also anticipated for her Wisconsin case. The filings aim to maintain the status quo in the states in order to give the Supreme Court time to consider the allegations presented in her lawsuits.
>
> "These cases raise constitutional issues and prove massive fraud."

But the Supreme Court eventually dismissed these cases too. On February 22, 2021, the US Supreme Court decided to dismiss five election cases. The left laughed and cheered the court's inaction. After deciding not to fast-track the cases, the justices rejected election challenges filed by President Donald Trump and his allies in five states President Joe Biden won: Arizona, Georgia, Michigan, Pennsylvania, and Wisconsin.[83]

Case after case went before Obama Judges or other judges who either threw them out or refused to hear them. Many of these cases were never taken up because the judges claimed the plaintiffs had no standing. But when an election

82 (Hoft J. , Sidney Powell Asks the Supreme Court to Intervene and Decertify States' Results in Michigan, Arizona, Georgia and Wisconsin, 2020)

83 (Press, 2021)

is stolen or has irregularities that the citizens believe impacted the election, who else has standing if not the aggrieved candidates or citizens?

65 Project

On the morning of January 6, 2021, Big Media reported that President Trump had lost all but one court case in efforts to address the stolen election. The data came from Hillary Clinton's former 2016 campaign attorney Marc Elias. Here is a portion of a report from *USA Today*:[84]

> President Donald Trump spent much of the 2020 presidential campaign insisting that he could only lose if the election was rigged against him, and he has spent nearly every day since his defeat claiming his dire predictions of fraud had come to pass.
>
> But just as he cried foul before a single vote was cast—something he also did in 2016—Trump has maintained he was robbed of victory without any credible evidence to support that belief.
>
> Despite assurances from his own departments of Justice and Homeland Security that no serious fraud occurred, Trump has raged against the election result and mounted a relentless campaign to reverse President-elect Joe Biden's 306–232 Electoral College win.
>
> The president, his lawyers, and his allies have filed scores of lawsuits; made repeated allegations of election fraud in news and social media; organized protests; tried to convince state legislatures to take action; and held hearings in various state houses, hotel ballrooms and, at one point, a landscaping company. And on Wednesday, 13 senators and more than 100 Republican lawmakers plan to object to the certification of Biden's win when Congress meets in a joint session.
>
> All those efforts to overturn the election can be a bit dizzying, so *USA TODAY* has broken it down by the numbers to help make sense of it all.

84 (William Cummings, 2021)

> The president and his allies filed 62 lawsuits in state and federal courts seeking to overturn election results in states the president lost, according to Marc Elias, a Democratic election lawyer who is tracking the outcomes.
>
> Out of the 62 lawsuits filed challenging the presidential election, 61 have failed, according to Elias.
>
> Some cases were dismissed for lack of standing and others based on the merits of the voter fraud allegations. The decisions have [come] from both Democratic-appointed and Republican-appointed judges—including federal judges appointed by Trump.
>
> State Supreme Courts in Arizona, Nevada, and Arizona each rejected or declined to hear Trump's appeals to overturn results in those states, while the Pennsylvania and Michigan supreme courts denied multiple lawsuits.
>
> The 60th and 61st losses came in recent days.

The article went on the show charts with 62 boxes, and all were colored blue but one. The message of the article using Elias as its source was clear—President Trump lost virtually all his lawsuits in his failed efforts to overturn the election.[85]

In early March of 2022, a group was created that targeted the attorneys who represented the cases that were filed in the courts after the 2022 election by President Trump and individuals close to him who believed the election had been stolen and wanted to prevent the stolen election from being certified.[86]

"65 Project" was created and named after what the group claimed were 65 frivolous cases that should not have been filed after the 2020 election [their rendition of the number of cases had increased since Jan 6]. *Influence Watch* reported on the "project" and pointed out that 65 Project was a campaign targeting lawyers who aided attempts by then-President Donald Trump and his supporters to address the fraud in the 2020 Election using far-left advertisements, threats

85 Ibid

86 (Watch, 2023)

of disbarment, and changing rules within the American Bar Association, ostensibly to deter future similar efforts.[87]

> The 65 Project was "devised" by Democratic consultant and former Clinton administration official Melissa Moss. It is a project of Law Works, a group with no website or public financial disclosures. The name "65 Project" refers to the number of lawsuits filed by supporters of President Donald Trump to overturn the 2020 presidential election.
>
> The 65 Project was launched to punish lawyers who supported President Trump and to dissuade future attempts to overturn elections on illegitimate grounds.
>
> According to the 65 Project, then-President Trump and a group of lawyers attempted to steal the 2020 presidential election by filing dozens of false lawsuits to disrupt the electoral process and permit Trump or his sympathizers to use their power to overturn the election results. The 65 Project refers to these lawyers as the "army of Big Lie Lawyers," a reference to the concept of a lie so ostentatious that people doubt it could be credibly fabricated, a principle credited to Second World War-era Nazi propaganda.

65 Project claimed to be bipartisan, but the group has yet to target any Democrats. One of the advisers to the project is David Brock, the founder of Media Matters for America.[88] This group has targeted conservative reporters and entities for years. The group uses techniques like doxing individuals in efforts that can cause them financial or reputational harm.

65 Project wasn't correct in its number of cases related to the 2020 Election and President Trump's race. It certainly wasn't accurate about the results as well.

87 Ibid

88 Ibid

The Real 2020 Election Case Count

Not only were there more than 65 cases related to the 2020 election, but also the actions taken by the court were much different from what Marc Elias and the left claimed. According to a file that was maintained by ElectionIntegrity.org[89], there were more than 80 cases that they tracked related to the 2020 Election. Here are the results of their analysis as of June of 2021:[90]

- There are 87 court cases to date based on the 2020 election
- In 26 cases, President Trump was the plaintiff
- In 56 cases, President Trump was not the plaintiff
- In 5 cases, President Trump is the defendant
- In 24 cases, the case was decided on the merits
- In 17 of the 24 cases (71%) decided on the merits, President Trump and/or the GOP prevailed
- 12 cases remained active at that time

The problem with the cases presented to the courts was not that the cases were weak or that they did not include enough support. The problem was that the judges decided in the majority of cases not to hear the cases. When the cases were heard and decided on the merits, President Trump prevailed 71 percent of the time.91

Professor and attorney David Clements shared in January 2021 the following about the election cases after the 2020 Election. This assertion has never changed:[92]

> For those who believe "there is no evidence, you don't know what you are talking about," he said. "I've reviewed hours upon hours of public

89 (Integrity, 2023)

90 (Hoft J. , Fraud Cases Shows 87 Total Cases – Trump and/or GOP Won 71% of Cases Where Merits Were Heard, 2021)

91 Ibid

92 (Hoft J. , Update on the BIG LIE: Law Professor Confirms Election Fraud Evidence Is "Significant" – Cases Only Dismissed on Process Grounds Not Merit, 2021)

hearings. I have read almost all of the lawsuits that are out there. Most of them were dismissed on legal process grounds."

These suits, he said, were dismissed due to a legal lack of standing. "The general argument" that was presented in these cases, he said, "was that because this was a general harm," then "you have no standing because your harm has to be particular. It's not because there isn't evidence. There is evidence," the professor emphasized.

Georgia Absentee Ballot Case

One case in Georgia was still ongoing at the time of this writing. It claimed that absentee ballots in the 2020 election identified during recounts in Fulton County were found to be in pristine shape. They hadn't been folded, which would have been necessary for them to have been mailed or received during the election. The ballots must have had corresponding envelopes, because the names, addresses and signatures on the envelopes are checked against records to ensure the ballots are from valid voters in the voter rolls.

Any ballots not folded could not have been mailed or handled inside an envelope and therefore must be invalid. The lawsuit asked that these 147,000 ballots be reviewed to determine their validity (the election in Georgia was awarded to Joe Biden three days after Election Day by a 12,000-ballot margin).[93]

This case was filed after the election. After holding hearings on the case during the ten months after the election, the judge eventually decided that the plaintiffs didn't have standing in the case, despite being local citizens and voters. This ruling was appealed to the Appellate Court, which agreed with the lower court. The case was then appealed to the Georgia Supreme Court.[94]

On December 20, 2022, more than two years after the election, the Georgia Supreme Court ruled that the petitioners in the case against Fulton

93 (Hoft J. , EXCLUSIVE: Tuesday's Georgia Supreme Court Ruling Will Likely Lead to Audit of 147,000 Suspected Fraudulent Ballots in Fulton County in the 2020 Election, 2022)

94 Ibid

County did have standing. The case was pushed back to the Appellate Court for reconsideration.[95]

It is expected that eventually, the petitioners will be granted their request years after the election. It's also expected that the ballots, if not tampered with since the initial review after the 2020 Election, will be found to be invalid. The result will be that Donald Trump would have won the election, and his rightful win will have been delayed for more than two years in Georgia.

President Trump received a record number of votes in the 2020 Election. Joe Biden was given the win in multiple states even though (as was established in *The Steal: Volume II – The Impossible Occurs*) massive corruption and criminal acts took place to give the election to Biden. The courts, contaminated with Obama judges and cowards, were either hell-bent on covering up for the crimes and unconstitutional acts in the election or were too frightened to do anything in the face of the politically driven Big Media, Big Tech, and politicians. As a result, the US court system at nearly every level sided with the lies, ignored the uncertifiable election being certified, and allowed a band of criminals to take over the White House and the multi-trillion-dollar US government.

95 (Lupo, 2022)

5

JAN 6

AFTER HAVING NUMEROUS unscrupulous events occur before, during, and after the 2020 Election, Americans who voted for President Trump had a right to be angry.

The entire country saw massive leads dissolve in the middle of the night and early in the morning after the election. They saw Americans being prevented from entering and observing election activities in numerous states when counting was going on. When observers complained nothing happened. When Americans went to the courts to receive orders to let them into the facilities where they were legally required to be, the courts may have obliged, but the local law enforcement didn't.

Then, after the fraudulent numbers were counted and certified, lawsuits with the courts were ignored or not heard. The courts used legal standing as their rationale to ignore the cases brought before them. All Americans have a standing in the Presidential election, but the courts didn't see it that way.

Court case after court case was thrown out or postponed. The rule of law was suddenly a thing of the past. The government let the good people in America down. Criminal activities were rewarded. The American people were forgotten. Their votes no longer counted.

This was a very pivotal point in US history. Would America have free and fair elections, or were bad actors going to choose the winners in American elections from this day forward?

This all led to the events of January 6, 2021.

Trump Capitol Rally and Speech

On December 19, 2020, President Trump announced on Twitter for the first time that he was holding a rally on January 6, 2021, in Washington DC.[96] This gave Americans plenty of time to make arrangements to be there. It also gave the Deep State plenty of time to plan for an event to further their insurrection.

The crowd that arrived that cold January 6th morning was massive. An estimated one million people showed up. Those who were there said it was the largest crowd they had ever seen[97] (The fact that Joe Biden received only a few hundred in attendance at his inauguration only two weeks later is more proof that Joe Biden didn't win a legitimate election in 2020).

After other speakers shared on stage at the Ellipse between the White House and the Washington Monument, President Trump arrived on stage, and he couldn't help but comment on the size of the crowd:[98]

> Well, thank you very much. This is incredible.
>
> Media will not show the magnitude of this crowd. Even I, when I turned on today, I looked, and I saw thousands of people here. But you don't see hundreds of thousands of people behind you because they don't want to show that.

96 (Trump, 2020)

97 (Hoft J. , FBI Is Looking to Arrest and Abuse 500 More of the 800 Individuals Who Entered the US Capitol on January 6 – Out of the One Million Who Saw Trump Speak, 2021)

98 (Naylor, 2021)

> We have hundreds of thousands of people here, and I just want them to be recognized by the fake news media. Turn your cameras please and show what's really happening out here, because these people are not going to take it any longer. They're not going to take it any longer. Go ahead. Turn your cameras, please. Would you show? They came from all over the world, actually, but they came from all over our country.
>
> I just really want to see what they do. I just want to see how they covered. I've never seen anything like it. But it would be really great if we could be covered fairly by the media. The media is the biggest problem we have as far as I'm concerned, single biggest problem. The fake news and the Big Tech.
>
> Big Tech is now coming into their own. We beat them four years ago. We surprised them. We took them by surprise, and this year, they rigged an election. They rigged it like they've never rigged an election before.

President Trump had no idea how bad it was. Two years later, the "censorship-industrial complex" was uncovered that was well in place on Jan 6 (this is discussed in Chapter 8). The government was working with NGOs, Big Media, and Big Tech to censor President Trump and conservative media.

President Trump continued:[99]

> All of us here today do not want to see our election victory stolen by emboldened radical-left Democrats, which is what they're doing. And stolen by the fake news media. That's what they've done and what they're doing. We will never give up. We will never concede. It doesn't happen. You don't concede when there's theft involved.
>
> Our country has had enough. We will not take it anymore, and that's what this is all about. And to use a favorite term that all of you people really came up with: We will stop the steal. Today, I will lay

99 Ibid

> out just some of the evidence proving that we won this election and we won it by a landslide. This was not a close election . . .
>
> And I was told by the real pollsters—we do have real pollsters—they know that we were going to do well and we were going to win. What I was told, if I went from 63 million, which we had four years ago, to 66 million, there was no chance of losing. Well, we didn't go to 66, we went to 75 million, and they say we lost. We didn't lose.
>
> And by the way, does anybody believe that Joe had 80 million votes? Does anybody believe that? He had 80 million computer votes. It's a disgrace. There's never been anything like that. You could take third-world countries. Just take a look. Take third-world countries. Their elections are more honest than what we've been going through in this country. It's a disgrace. It's a disgrace.

President Trump went on to praise Rudy Giuliani, John Eastman, the police, and the Secret Service. He thanked everyone for being there and encouraged Mike Pence to do the right thing, although Pence wasn't there; he was down the hill inside the Capitol Building. Then he shared the purpose of the gathering:[100]

> We're gathered together in the heart of our nation's capital for one very, very basic and simple reason: To save our democracy.

President Trump went on to discuss all the fraudulent and suspicious actions and results identified in the 2020 election. He went on for what seemed to be more than an hour as he discussed Hunter Biden and the election and more. It was a very cold January day, and yet, the million Americans on hand stayed until he was finished.

America was in the hands of Vice President Mike Pence. The President and the American people hoped that Pence was going to do the right thing. Then, during President Trump's speech, while the President and a million followers

100 Ibid

were at the Ellipse, with the Washington Monument in the background, Pence released a statement.

VICE PRESIDENT MIKE PENCE

After all the corruption, lies, and manufactured results, and after the courts dismissed or ignored the numerous cases before them related to the 2020 Election, there was still hope. The one last action that could be taken was to not certify the uncertifiable results from the 2020 election and send them back to the states for review.

This could be done, per some legal experts, if the Vice President found it necessary to challenge the results in certain states. Seven states provided two sets of electors to Washington DC for certification on January 6, 2021. These states were Wisconsin, Michigan, Pennsylvania, Georgia, Arizona, Nevada, and New Mexico.[101]

All these states had numerous issues in the 2020 Election that led to the two sets of electors. The hope was that Vice President Pence would either choose the electors who backed President Trump's election win, and the election would be over; or Pence would accept neither of the Trump or Biden electors and send the results back to the states, where the states would decide which set of electors would represent these states in the electoral college vote.[102]

Another option was that Pence would decide to move the election to the House because of the duplicate sets of electors, and each state would receive one vote for president. Because there are more Republican-led states, it was hoped that President Trump would win the election and overcome the massive fraud this way. The final option for Pence was to accept the Biden delegates and give the uncertifiable election to Biden.[103]

101 (Hoft J. , These Seven States Provided Two Sets of Electors to the US Congress – Tomorrow We See How They Will Be Handled, 2021)

102 Ibid

103 Ibid

At 9:00 a.m., as the day's events were getting underway in Washington DC, the world was watching to see if Pence would be a hero. President Trump tweeted:[104]

> If Vice President @Mike_Pence comes through for us, we will win the Presidency. Many States want to decertify the mistake they made in certifying incorrect & even fraudulent numbers in a process NOT approved by their State Legislatures (which it must be). Mike can send it back!

Vice President Pence would burn his name into the history books. He would either be a hero and the courageous man who stood up against the lies behind the stolen 2020 Election, or he would go down as a modern-day Brutus. Americans who were following the election knew that this was a historic day.[105]

Then, while President Trump was speaking at the Ellipse, his Vice President, Mike Pence, released a statement on what he had decided to do that day. His statement was three pages long, indicating that Pence had been working on this for some time. If he was telling the President that he didn't know what he was going to do, it was clear that this was not true.[106]

In his statement Pence began with a number of paragraphs about the history behind what he was going to do and his interpretation of the Constitution. Then Pence finally shared, "It is my considered judgement that my oath to support and defend the Constitution constrains me from claiming unilateral authority to determine which electoral votes should be counted and which should not." Looking back, this really made no sense. Pence "folded like a lawn chair."[107]

---

104 (Hoft J. , Today In a Matter of Minutes – Vice President Pence Will Become Known in History as a Hero or a Traitor – Which Will It Be?, 2021)

105 Ibid

106 (Laila, BREAKING: Pence Releases Statement Ahead of Certification of Electoral College, Says He Will NOT Block Biden's Electors, 2021)

107 (Laila, BREAKING: Pence Releases Statement Ahead of Certification of Electoral College, Says He Will NOT Block Biden's Electors, 2021)

Immediately, Pence was looked at in a new light. The fact that he shared this while the President was speaking in front of a million supporters was terrible timing and a knife in the back of President Trump and America. Suddenly, the many Trump haters who Pence brought into the White House over the prior four years were looked at as Pence plants. Also, Pence's actions in encouraging President Trump to remove General Michael Flynn from the White House early in his administration became glaringly suspect. Pence was now and will forevermore be looked upon as a turncoat to President Trump and the largest political base in history.[108]

Pence showed up at the Capitol as the House and Senate gathered to begin the certification process of the 2020 Election. Pence looked sheepish, like a little child who knew he was doing something wrong. Speaker Pelosi called the meeting to order a little after 1:00 p.m. locally, and then Pence began the certification process for the 2020 Presidential election. Almost immediately, Senator Ted Cruz from Texas and Representative Paul Gosar from Arizona challenged Arizona's 2020 Election results.[109]

The House and Senate members then split up to discuss the challenges with Arizona's results. GOP Senate Minority Leader Mitch McConnell was given the opportunity to discuss the election, and he argued:[110]

> "Voters, the courts, and the states have all spoken—they've all spoken," he said. "If we overrule them, it would damage our republic forever."

McConnell hated President Trump and was willing to do anything to see him removed from office. At times, McConnell looked like he had stronger ties to China than America.

A few minutes after McConnell spoke, small packages were located at the RNC and DNC headquarters near the Capitol. These packages were later

---

108 (Hoft J. , Pence Betrayed General Flynn in 2017 and Today He Betrayed President Trump and America, 2021)

109 (Durkee, 2021)

110 (Kat Lonsdorf, 2022)

confirmed to be pipe bombs. A few minutes later, Vice President Pence was escorted from the Senate floor, and then Pelosi was removed from the House floor. Minutes after that, the House and Senate were called to recess.[111]

THE CAPITOL RIOTS

Big Media reported that the reason that the Capitol was cleared on Jan 6 was because of the assault on the Capitol by Trump supporters, but Capitol Police Chief Steven Sund testified before the Senate in February 2021 that the two congressional buildings, the Cannon House Office Building, as well as one of the Library of Congress buildings were evacuated due to the discovery of the pipe bombs.[112]

A report prepared by a Congressional Committee that investigated the events on January 6, the "Jan 6 Committee" report was released in late December 2022. This report barely mentioned the pipe bombs, and it neglected to mention that the pipe bomber left his bombs at the RNC and DNC headquarters on the evening of January 5th, not the 6th. After more than two years, the FBI found no leads on the bomber, and the Jan 6 Committee didn't seem to care.[113]

For the next few hours on Jan 6, the Big Media was all over the story at the Capitol. The corporate news wasn't interested in any mention of the election steal; it was interested in the chaos at the Capitol. President Trump had offered to send in National Guard troops before January 6th, but Speaker Pelosi and Washington DC Mayor Muriel Bowser declined the offer.[114]

In addition, Sund, the former chief of US Capitol Police, said security officials at the House and Senate rebuffed his early requests to call in the National Guard ahead of a demonstration in support of President Trump. Sund also reported that he requested National Guard troops throughout the day but was

111 Ibid

112 (Hoft J. , IT WAS ALL A LIE: Congress Was Evacuated on Jan. 6 Due to Pipe Bomb Threat — Not Because of Trump Supporters Walking Halls, 2021)

113 (Hoft J. , Jan 6 Report Hides Any Mention of Pipe Bomber Who Was Cause of Shutting Down Congress That Day, 2022)

114 (Smith, 2021)

rebuffed. National Guard troops didn't arrive until three hours after the initial riots started outside the Capitol.[115]

According to a report unearthed in March of 2023 that was considered classified by the Deep State DOJ and kept from the American people, the Washington DC police knew that there was going to be a large crowd on that day, and they prepared for the event. Notably, the Capitol Police allowed for multiple anti-Trump events at the Capitol on the same day. One of these groups was Antifa—the violent group involved in numerous riots across the country during the summer of 2020.[116]

Before President Trump finished his speech at the Ellipse, there was a large crowd brewing at the Capitol. Americans were upset with the election activities that led to the Joe Biden certification, but offsetting this was the very cold weather. Many people went to the Capitol expecting to see Vice President Pence send the delegates back to the states or hoping to see President Trump win out in a vote in Congress. Instead, Pence released his decision to certify the election for Joe Biden, which sent many people home after the President's speech. They were depressed and cold. Nevertheless, there still was a massive crowd that walked down to the Capitol that day.

There was no signage that said keep out and no noticeable fencing to hold people back from going into the Capitol. Many people walked into the Capitol and out without any idea that what they were doing was wrong. These people were later targeted and arrested for trespassing at the Capitol. Many of these good Americans were charged with crimes related to domestic terrorism or even sedition. This was hardly the case for many who entered the Capitol, a large percentage who were invited in by the Capitol Police.

Video released two years later by Tucker Carlson on FOX News showed that most the protesters in the Capitol that day were wandering around showing reverence for the building that they were in. The police looked more

---

115 (Diaz, 2021)

116 (Hoft J. , HUGE: "THEY LIED ABOUT EVERYTHING" – 96-Page DC Police Report UNCOVERED – Shows Govt Knew MAGA Was Coming on Jan 6 and Entrapped Them ALL, 2023)

like chaperons than anything else as they showed people around inside the building.[117]

One individual that Big Media claimed was violent and dangerous in the Capitol that day was Jacob Chansley, the "QAnon Shaman," as he was referred to in the press. Chansley was dressed in furs and a hat with horns and had body paint on his face and shirtless body. Chansley was eventually sentenced to 41 months in prison for his "crimes." But Tucker Carlson showed that nine policemen were right next to Chansley at various times on Jan 6. They escorted him throughout the Capitol, and he harmed no one and committed no damage to the building. Chansley actually said a prayer in the Capitol. The media and the Jan 6 Committee lied about Chansley being violent.[118]

A few nights later in March of 2023, Tucker Carlson released video of another "Jan 6er" who was arrested for his actions on that day. Daniel Goodwyn walked inside the Capitol on Jan 6 and was told almost immediately to leave by a Capitol policeman. He obliged and turned around and walked out. He was in the Capitol for literally less than a minute. He was later charged for domestic terrorism and trespassing and, as of March 2023, was facing a year in prison.

Goodwyn said he wasn't a "political prisoner." After spending a month in jail and then a year under house arrest, he said political prisoners have rights. He was a "political hostage."[119] After the Biden regime took over and his DOJ was in place, they made hundreds of arrests related to hundreds of cases like Daniel Goodwyn.

There was violence at the Capitol on Jan 6, which was unusual, since no incidents of violence were reported at the numerous 2020 Trump rallies prior to that day. President Trump attracted 1.1 million Trump supporters to his rallies in the fall of 2020 with no damage or violence reported.

---

117 (Hoft J. , BREAKING: Tucker Carlson Releases Video Showing Capitol Police Escorting Jacob Chansley "QAnon Shaman" Peacefully Through the Capitol (VIDEO), 2023)

118 Ibid

119 (Hoft J. , "Jan. 6 I Think Is Probably Second Only to the 2020 Election as the Biggest Scam in My Lifetime" – Tucker During Interview with Jan 6 "Political Hostage" Daniel Goodwyn, 2023)

Damages to the Capitol on Jan 6, mostly in the form of broken glass windows and the like, totaled $1.5 million. This paled in comparison to the estimated over $1 billion in damages incurred in the Black Lives Matter riots in the summer of 2020. In Minneapolis alone, over 1,500 businesses were destroyed that summer. Over 700 police were injured in the BLM riots across the country in 2020 as well, while a reported 114 officers were injured on Jan 6 at the Capitol.[120]

There definitely were riots outside the Capitol on Jan 6. Capitol Police were blamed for inciting some of the riots, while Trump supporters or individuals embedded with Trump supporters were violent as well. Big Media was all over the violence that took place and used it for years to promote their narrative that Trump supporters were violent.

In addition to non-stop reporting on the violent acts of Jan 6 against the police outside the Capitol, for more than two years, the Democrats and Big Media reported that five police officers lost their lives that day at the Capitol. This was repeated over and over. On January 6, 2023, two years after Jan 6, Joe Biden and House Minority Leader Hakeem Jeffries claimed that five Capitol Police officers lost their lives on Jan 6. But this was simply not true. No Capitol Police lost their lives that day.[121]

Tucker Carlson discussed Hakeem Jeffrey's comments on his show on the evening of January 6, 2023:[122]

> Five heroic officers were lost, he said. It's almost impossible to believe that adults could stand behind him as he said that, because everyone in the picture you just saw knows that is not true. It's not a stilted interpretation of events. It's a flat out lie. No police officers were killed on January 6, period.

---

120 (Hoft J. , JAN 6 REMEMBERED: Confirmed: Jan. 6 Protest Resulted in Estimated $1.5 Million in Damages — Or 1/1000th of Damages by Black Lives Matter-Antifa Protests in 2020, 2022)

121 (Hoft J. , Tucker Carlson Discusses Relentless Media Lies About Jan 6 Protests on Second Anniversary of Historic Day, 2023)

122 Ibid

Four Americans did die at the Capitol on Jan 6, but they weren't police officers; they were all Trump supporters.

THE JAN 6 COMMITTEE

The Jan 6 Committee released its report after two years of the most radical show trial in US history. This House Committee was composed of mostly Democrats and two Never-Trumper Republicans who hated President Trump—Liz Cheney and Adam Kinzinger. Cheney is the daughter of former Vice President Dick Cheney who President Trump called out numerous times for his efforts in getting America into the Afghanistan and Iraqi wars. Kinzinger was just always vocal about his opposition to President Trump.

The Jan 6 Committee was created by the Democrat-led House to investigate the events at the Capitol. But when the GOP picked five members to be on the Committee, Speaker Nancy Pelosi unilaterally changed the makeup and participants on the committee, allowing only Cheney and Kinzinger to participate from the GOP side of the isle. Pelosi's actions officially made the Jan 6 committee an American show trial.[123]

Attorney Mark Levin discussed Pelosi's Jan 6 Committee on his *FOX News* Show in May of 2022:[124]

> The "Life, Liberty & Levin" host made the case that Democrats in Congress had abused their powers and colluded with the media to take down the former president because they view him as a potential 2024 threat.
>
> He listed three Democrat-elected prosecutors who had targeted the Trump Organization for purely political motives, before he laid into the "so-called January 6 Committee" as a "Stalinist" "farce."

123 (Laila, New: GOP Leader McCarthy Pulls His 5 Republican Members From Jan. 6 Committee After Pelosi Rejects Jordan, Banks, 2021)

124 (Hoft J. , Mark Levin on FOX News Calls the Jan 6 Committee "A Front Politburo Type Committee Set Up by Nancy Pelosi...Very Stalinist in its Makeup", 2022)

> "[It's] nothing more than a front politburo type committee set up by Nancy Pelosi loaded with the most radical leftist Democrats you can imagine and two of the worst never-Trumper reprobates that you can imagine. There's not a single lawyer on that committee's staff, not a single representative on the committee's staff to raise any objections to what that committee is doing. It is very Stalinist in its makeup," he said.
>
> Levin also called the committee a "farce" that was "violating the Constitution," because it was beyond Congress's power to conduct criminal investigations.

When the farce was completed due to the change in House leadership after the 2022 mid-term election, the Jan 6 Committee released its report. After more than a year of this kangaroo court, the most important topic about the Jan 6 riots was noticeably missing—the death of four Trump supporters on Jan 6.

Death at the Capitol

On January 6, 2021, an estimated million people arrived in Washington DC to see what they hoped was the Constitution working as the founders had intended. These Americans knew that the 2020 Election never should have been certified for Joe Biden and they hoped to see the certified results for Biden overturned. America had just suffered through a COVID-19 nightmare and an Election nightmare, and the majority of Americans were ready for a win.

The President spoke, and during his speech, as noted above, the Vice President announced that he was going to certify Joe Biden for President. This was a tremendous slap in the face to Americans and the US Constitution.

Many Trump supporters walked down to the Capitol, and a huge crowd was on hand outside the building. It was very cold so many individuals returned to their hotel rooms, cars, and homes, but thousands stayed and walked down to the Capitol.

Suddenly, without warning, the Capitol Police—or individuals dressed up like Capitol Police—began firing rubber bullets, flash grenades, and smoke bombs on the crowd. Women, the elderly, and children were in the crowd. Two older Trump supporters were in the crowd as well. Both middle-aged men were peacefully standing in the crowd when suddenly with no warning grenades, bombs, and bullets began flying.[125]

Kevin Greeson and Benjamin Phillips died that day. They were killed without warning. It's believed they had heart attacks when flash grenades suddenly blew up in their faces. These men had arrived in DC to meet with other Trump supporters and support their President. They never made it home.[126]

Rosanne Boyland drove to Washington DC that day with a friend. She was a young lady with a special talent. She was a recovering addict who worked as a drug counselor. For seven years, she attended meetings in her local community and did what she could to help others with the same issues and addictions. She also was a Trump supporter.[127]

Boyland found herself caught between the crowd outside the Capitol and Capitol Police when the madness began. Trump supporters were on a set of steps outside the Capitol when Capitol Police began pushing the crowd on top of innocent Americans on the steps.

Boyland and the crowd of Trump supporters were pushed by police down the steps and under a ceiling-high, bone-crushing, and deadly pile that cops doused with opulent amounts of pepper spray and teargas. The police would not allow anyone to help the individuals being crushed, and they attacked anyone who tried to help. After about ten long minutes, the protesters were able to work themselves out of the pile and save each other.[128]

Boyland lay motionless on the steps after the pile finally cleared. People were unable to get near her to help, and it was then that she was seen being beaten brutally by Police Officer Lila Morris with a stick multiple times. Morris beat Boyland so hard and so many times that she lost her stick![129]

---

125 (Hoft J. , Trump Supporters Killed by Police That Day – And Only Mention Ashli Babbitt in Passing – And No Mention of Attempted Murder of Derrick Vargo Who Was Pushed Off 2-Story Ledge by Police, 2022)

126 Ibid

127 (Castronuova, 2021)

128 (Hoft J. , EXPLOSIVE NEW VIDEO of Rosanne Boyland Shows Police Attempting to Revive Her in Trash-Filled Hall, Police Say She Was "Trampled" – Then Later They Lied and Said She Died of Overdose (VIDEO), 2023)

129 Ibid

Boyland's face was blue and bloody as her body lay motionless. Men tried to help and defend her, only to be tear-gassed or struck by police themselves. People begged and pleaded with police to give Boyland CPR, but the police ignored these calls. The men finally carried Boyland down the stairs away from the attacks of police to attempt administer CPR themselves.[130]

Ronald McAbee, a Sheriff from Tennessee, was one of the men who worked on Boyland. He unbuttoned Boyland's pants and removed her belt to access the femoral artery in her leg and take a pulse. As of this writing, McAbee still sits in pre-trial detention for the January 6 crime of trying to save Rosanne Boyland. Over a dozen men sit in pre-trial detention who were helping Rosanne or reacting to her death. It's as if authorities are keeping them behind bars to prevent them from sharing their stories and what they saw on Jan 6.[131]

The Capitol coroner announced to Big Media that Boyland had died from a drug overdose. Next, the government cremated her body so the family could not see it. Boyland's family was unable to perform a secondary autopsy and to this day has not been provided their daughter's full autopsy report. This woman who helped so many recover from their addictions was slandered by her government and labeled a drug addict, all because she supported her President.[132]

Officer Lila Morris, as of the date of this writing, still walks the halls of Congress—a hero.[133]

Another Trump supporter was shot and killed in cold blood on January 6, 2021, inside the Capitol. Ashli Babbitt was gunned down inside the US Capitol. She was only 98 pounds, posed no threat and had no weapons.[134]

Months later, after keeping his name hidden from the public, Lt. Mike Byrd was exonerated for killing Ashli Babbitt. Byrd gave no warning, he ran

---

130 Ibid

131 Ibid

132 Op cit, Castronuova

133 (Hoft J. , NEVER FORGET: Capitol Police Gassed and Beat Trump Supporter Rosanne Boyland til She Died — Then The Government Cremated Her Body So Her Family Could Not See Her Bloody Wounds, 2022)

134 (Hoft J. , Biden Regime Spent Tens of Thousands of Dollars to House Ashli Babbitt's Killer Mike Byrd in Special "Distinguished Visitor Suite" After He Murdered Ashli, 2023)

from the scene of the crime, he shot an unarmed woman dead who posed no threat. And now he walks free.[135]

We then learned that Lt. Mike Byrd was reportedly never interviewed before he was exonerated for killing Ashli Babbitt. Not only that, but Judicial Watch released documents that revealed the US Air Force spent tens of thousands of taxpayer dollars to House Mike Byrd in a "distinguished visitor suite" after he murdered Ashli Babbitt in cold blood.[136]

The Jan 6 report doesn't even mention the deaths of Greeson, Phillips, or Boyland. It barely mentions the death of Ashli Babbitt, with a note on p. 665 that says:[137]

> "Members of Congress can be seen evacuating through the Speaker's Lobby when a USCP officer fatally shot Ashli Babbitt at 2:44 p.m."

The Jan 6 Committee had no intention of being objective and independent in its investigation into the events of January 6, 2021, at the US Capitol. They weren't interested in the truth. They only wanted to punish Trump supporters and indict President Trump after pinning him to the Capitol violence on that day.

ANTIFA, AZOV BATTALION, AND THE DEEP STATE

Big Media has to date portrayed the violent events on Jan 6 at the Capitol as acts committed by Trump supporters. However, on that day, the events appeared suspicious, because President Trump had 1.1 million people at his rallies with no violence reported at all.

135 Ibid

136 Ibid

137 Op cit, Trump supporters killed by police that day...

The longer you look at the events on Jan 6 and the actual reports of events on that day, the more it becomes clear that there may never have been any violence that day if not for instigators and anti-Trump actors in the crowd.

We know Antifa, the violent anti-American group that was responsible for the destruction of US cities in the summer of 2020, was at the Capitol. As noted above, the police knew that Antifa had scheduled an event outside the Capitol on Jan 6.

The Antifa event at the Capitol that day was advertised ahead of time. Utah Antifa member John Solomon set up an Antifa event that day. He was caught on video bragging about posing as a Trump supporter and breaking a window at the US Capitol during the riots.[138]

Solomon claimed that he wasn't an Antifa member but only filmed Antifa members at events. However, it was determined that he was a leader of the Utah Antifa-BLM movement and was previously arrested in Utah.[139]

Solomon also videotaped the events at the Capitol on Jan 6 and was a guest on *CNN* to discuss the riots. He ended up spending one day in jail for being in the Capitol on Jan 6, but it was worth it, as he was paid $35,000 from both *CNN* and *NBC* for the video coverage he provided that day.[140]

This video was later used by the Democrats in their second bogus impeachment of President Trump. How ironic that the Democrats used video from Antifa to support their accusations that President Trump was behind the riots on Jan 6.[141]

---

138 (Hoft J. , NEVER FORGET: Antifa-BLM Leader Who Was Filmed Inside US Capitol on Jan. 6, Broke a Window, and Organized Antifa Rally Near Capitol That Day – ONLY SPENT ONE DAY IN JAIL, 2022)

139 Ibid

140 (Hoft J. , UPDATE: BLM-Antifa Organizer John Sullivan, Who Was Arrested After Storming US Capitol, Bashing Windows Is Writing a Book, Being Paid for Video as Trump Supporters Rot in Jail, 2021)

141 (Hoft J. , Someone Tell President Trump's Attorneys – The Democrats' Footage Showing Violence at the Capitol on January 6th Was Filmed by Antifa, 2021)

There was ample evidence that Antifa was at the Jan 6 event at the Capitol that day. Later, videos and social media posts were uncovered showing Antifa activists storming the Capitol and bragging about it.[142]

Looking back, it was an international affair of Deep State actors at the Capitol on Jan 6. XRVision identified in near real-time Ukrainian political operators on Jan 6 at the Capitol building and successfully traced their network. Other reports mistakenly identified these individuals as Russians at first, as if they were there to provide a narrative that Russians supporting President Trump were present that day to riot at the Capitol. Two years later, as the Russia–Ukraine war broke out, Americans became better acquainted with this Nazi related group (the Ukrainian Azov Battalion).[143]

Overall, however, when looking back at that day, the largest group present at the Capitol to create and cause violence was the Deep State actors working for the FBI, the DOJ, or other three-lettered government entities.

Two years after his imprisonment, word came out about a Jan 6 hostage by the name of Jeffrey McKellop, a decorated former 3rd Special Forces Group soldier and US government contractor. Jeffrey was being held in the DC Gulag in Washington DC as a political prisoner after he served his country for 22 years of military service (the DC Gulag was the name given to the Washington DC jail where the Jan 6 hostages were being held).[144]

> Jeffrey has been silenced by his government. After his arrest in March 2021, Jeffrey delved into video footage and documented evidence from January 6. Jeffrey was able to identify numerous government informants and agitators in the massive Trump crowd that day. After he put together his evidence, he sent it out to numerous contacts. That was when the FBI came into his prison cell and took his research. They

142 (Hoft J. , IGNORED BY MEDIA AND FBI: Antifa-BLM Activists Are Posting Photos and Bragging Online About Storming US Capitol on Jan. 6, 2021)

143 (Hoft J. , Why Were Ukrainian Nazis in the U.S. Capitol on January 6?, 2022)

144 (Hoft J. , HE HAS THE PROOF: DC Gulag Political Prisoner and Decorated Army Special Forces Soldier Jeffrey McKellop Reveals Extent of Government Agents at J6 Capitol Protest – IT WAS A COMPLETE SET-UP! (Audio), 2023)

> then attempted to silence him and banned him from phone and mail privileges . . .
>
> . . . [McKellop says] I know for a fact that there were undercover agents, man. I saw them. I spotted it. And when you find one, then you know what to look for, and then you find them. All undercover agents, they all wear the same thing. They all move the same way. They all get together the same way. Why do I know these? Because I used to do the same thing . . .
>
> I've been saying this for a year and a half now, that Antifa were there, Antifa and BLM were there, but they changed their chameleons, man. They look like us, they dress like us, they act like us, and then they committed violence in our name. That is guerrilla warfare.

McKellop identified individuals in the videos he saw, and he is convinced these people were working for the government. He's been in jail for more than two years without a trial for the crime of knowing too much.[145]

There were numerous individuals identified after Jan 6 who were clearly working for someone. One individual by the name of Ray Epps was the most well-known agitator at the Capitol on Jan 6. Many people believe that he was there not to protest the stolen election but to instigate riots on that day.

Epps was identified the night before Jan 6 at an event standing next to Antifa member John Sullivan. There are pictures of them standing together. Epps was reportedly saying that we are going to go into the Capitol on Jan 6.[146]

He was then identified at the Capitol on January 6 leading efforts to get past not one but two police blockades. After Jan 6, he was on the FBI's Most Wanted List from January 8 through July 1, and then he suddenly was removed with no explanation.[147]

---

145 Ibid

146 (Hoft J. , Back on June 18 Gateway Pundit Was First to Report on Deep State Plant Ray Epps at the J-6 Protests — Today the Ray Epps Story Finally Made the Mainstream Daily Mail, 2021)

147 Ibid

At one point on Jan 6, Epps was seen pushing a large Trump sign at the police. Eight other Trump supporters were near him doing the same. These eight individuals are all serving years in prison for this act while Ray Epps walks free. Today, Ray Epps is still free.[148]

For every eight Trump supporters wrongly accused, placed in jail for years, charged with outrageous crimes, and placed in prison for years, there's a Ray Epps running around free.

Congress Reconvenes

After Congress reconvened later in the evening of Jan 6, the vote was taken on the 2020 Election. Joe Biden was certified as the winner of the 2020 Election, but even after the day's events, 147 Republican lawmakers, Representatives, and Senators still objected to the results of the 2020 Election.[149]

This vote was able to take place because Nancy Pelosi took over the proceedings. Looking back, some people believe that the crisis at the Capitol earlier in the day was necessary to make this vote happen, and an "emergency" was required on Jan 6 to prevent the 2020 election coup from being uncovered.[150]

A proposition that was laid out a couple of years after Jan 6. This theory suggests that the only way to prevent Congress from delaying the certification of state electoral votes was to create a crisis that could easily be designated as an emergency. And so, a crisis was created to eliminate motions to halt the certification of the election and investigate voting irregularities and fraud. When motions were eliminated from the records of the House, they could certify the fraud with no detractors on record. This would also provide the Supreme Court a reason to claim that any cases before it lacked standing.[151]

148 (Hoft J. , Ray Epps Lied – He Committed Criminal Acts and It Was ALL CAUGHT on Video — Here Are the Eight Trump Supporters the FBI Arrested and Who Are Serving Years in Prison for Committing Same Act, 2023)

149 (Zhou, 2021)

150 (Hoft J. , EXPLOSIVE: The 2020 Election Steal Required an "Emergency" on Jan 6 to Complete the Coup, 2023)

151 Ibid

In order to prevent motions challenging the election from being recorded in the Congressional record, the Speaker of the House, the Minority Leaders, and the President of the Congress (VP Pence) could not be present in the Chambers. This would be necessary to allow Speaker Pelosi to suspend Congress unilaterally under emergency rules.[152]

The crisis invoked emergency procedures, and Pelosi was able to prevent the delay of certification herself. When Congress returned later that night, Pelosi was in charge, and she initiated the NEW session under special emergency rules. The only purpose of the new session was to expedite the certification of the 2020 Election and dismiss all prior regular session procedural rules. This new session prevented any motions to consider a debate and pause the certification of state vote electors.[153]

This effort was very organized and carefully planned. It's likely most members of the House were quite aware of how the certification was going to be managed. New rules were created through the emergency crisis that occurred that afternoon. The Jan 6 riots ensured that no one was going to stop the certification of Joe Biden for President.

152 Ibid

153 Ibid

6

THE AUDITS

IN THE STEAL – Volume II: The Impossible Occurs, it was pointed out that for an auditor to provide an opinion on a set of numbers or a particular process, the final results, processes to obtain those results, and systems involved must be audited.

If the auditee prevents anyone from auditing the processes performed in the audit, and if management is reluctant to provide transparency on how the results were derived, the auditor overseeing the engagement would at minimum provide a qualified opinion on the results, noting those areas of contention and stating that accurate results could not be determined because key elements within the scope of the audit were not available to audit.

One of the first steps that an auditor takes when performing an audit is to determine the overall picture of the area or scope under audit. The results of this exercise will indicate which areas or processes should be investigated and focused on (the many anomalies that were evident after the 2020 Election indicated that the entire election needed to be reviewed).

After an auditor determines the overall scope of the audit, the processes, policies, systems, activities, regulations, and individuals involved are determined. The first major task after obtaining the overall results is to obtain documentation and inventories of data that support the results.

A good auditor will understand that ballots are valuable. The winner of an election with the most votes has the power to start wars or surrender borders. The leader of the United States can destroy the US and world economies or create changes that unleash economic growth around the world. The entire world is impacted by the winner of the US presidential election, so it is very important that the true winner is awarded the election.

Ballots should be treated like money. As a bank auditor, I was present after several bank robberies had taken place at branch locations in a large Midwestern city. I once met a young teller, her first week on the job, who shook uncontrollably after a robber came in, pointed a gun at her, and demanded she give him all her money. I arrived an hour after the event, and she was still shaking. My job as an auditor was to count all the money and determine how much the robber got away with and how much money was left. I learned that people would commit dangerous criminal acts for relatively small amounts of money. We learned in 2020 what people will do for global control.

I learned that money is valuable, and therefore, it needs to be protected and well controlled. It should be counted and reconciled, often under dual control (i.e., the presence of two individuals). Money shouldn't be lying around on tables or chairs. Money should be locked up throughout the day and at night. Video cameras should always be used to identify suspicious activities of individuals in and around the bank. Periodic audits should take place.

Money and ballots are similar in that both should be protected with the utmost care. You wouldn't leave money lying around on tables in a bank with teller drawers open, and ballots shouldn't be thrown about all over the place as well. Ballots should be locked up, and any activities related to ballots should be performed under dual controls (two people involved) and signed off on.154

This didn't happen in the 2020 Election. Videos were sometimes not working or not present. Ballots were thrown about everywhere. The entire election was a mess. These results required audits at a minimum. Ultimately, the results were not certifiable, and the elections should have been done over.

After having numerous shady and fraudulent events occur before, during, and after the 2020 Election, Americans who voted for President Trump wanted the results audited.

154 Hoft J., IMPORTANT FACT: Money and Ballots Are Valuable, That's Why You Ensure Every Penny and Every Ballot Is Valid When Auditing These Precious Items, 2021.

The entire country saw massive leads dissolve in the middle of the night and early in the morning after the election. They saw Americans being prevented from entering and observing election activities in numerous states when counting was going on. When observers complained, nothing happened. When Americans went to the courts to receive orders to let them into the facilities where they were legally required to be, the courts may have obliged, but the local law enforcement didn't.

Audits were demanded across the country. There was no way the guy who hid in his basement (who couldn't fill 12 circles at his "rallies" before the 2020 Election) received over 80 million votes. No way.

MICHIGAN

After the 2020 election, there were multiple questions concerning the results in Michigan and across the country. In one small county—Antrim County, Michigan—we saw one of the first audits of the 2020 Election.

Irregularities were identified in Antrim County in its 2020 Presidential election results that appeared to involve its machines. Only three days after the 2020 election, the county had identified thousands of votes that were incorrectly given to Joe Biden that should have been recorded as votes for President Trump. The county addressed these votes and rightly awarded the county for President Trump.[155]

A "system glitch" was recorded in the county. Similar glitches were identified across the country daily at that point in time. Eventually, these glitches led to the discovery of what was referred to as the "Drop and Roll" that was identified and discussed in *The Steal - Volume II: The Impossible Occurs.*[156]

As a result of this glitch, an audit was requested of Antrim County's 2020 Election results. On November 23, 2020, attorney Matthew DePerno

155 (Hoft J. , Antrim County in Michigan, Where First System 'Glitch' In 2020 Election Was Identified, Decides Not to Use Dominion Voting Machines in Upcoming May Election, 2021)

156 (Hoft J. , "Drop and Roll" — How The 2020 Election Was Stolen From President Donald Trump (Video), 2020)

of DePerno Law filed a lawsuit on behalf of a Central Lake resident against Antrim County, Michigan. Michigan's corrupt Democrat Secretary of State Jocelyn Benson blamed the vote switch from President Trump to Biden on the local Antrim County Clerk Sheryl Guy, claiming this was a "clerical" error.[157]

Guy had reported after the election that her team and several other Antrim County officials, when faced with inaccurate general election results on the day after the election, spent the next three very long days attempting to correct them, which they were finally able to do late Friday night, after starting over completely. They were finally able to certify the results at 10:00 p.m. Friday night.[158]

On December 4, 2020, 13th Circuit Court Judge Kevin A. Elsenheimer granted permission to a team of IT experts to conduct a forensic study of the 16 Dominion voting machines, tabulators, thumb drives, related software, and the clerk's "master tabulator" in Antrim County. Matthew DePerno quickly contacted the team of seven highly trained forensic IT experts he had assembled to perform the audit, and they agreed to arrive the following day to conduct the forensic examination. Within eight hours, the team gathered all they came for, and the collection was complete.[159]

Ten days later, on December 14, following a Zoom call hearing that included lawyers representing Secretary of State Benson (who injected herself into the case), attorney Matt DePerno was granted permission by Judge Elsenheimer to make the results public. Deperno's report shared the following:[160]

> After the forensic examination of 16 Dominion Voting machines in Antrim Co., MI, Allied Security Operations Group has concluded that the **Dominion Voting machines were assigned a 68.05% error rate**. DePerno explained that when ballots are put through the machine, a whopping 68.05% error rate means that 68.05% of the ballots are sent for bulk adjudication, which means they collect

157 (McMurray, 2021)

158 Ibid

159 Ibid

160 Ibid

the ballots in a folder. "The ballots are sent somewhere where people in another location can change the vote," DePerno explained. **The allowable election error rate established by the Federal Election Commission guidelines is 1 in 250,000 ballots or .0008%.**

Based on the Allied Security Operations report, Constitutional Attorney Matthew DePerno states: "We conclude that The Dominion Voting System should not be used in Michigan. We further conclude that the results of Antrim County should not have been certified.

No one was charged with a crime related to the system glitch in Antrim County. No one was indicted.

NEW HAMPSHIRE

The results in New Hampshire in the 2020 Presidential Election made no sense. New Hampshire was one of the many states whose results were suspect.[161]

- Republicans flipped the New Hampshire Senate from 14–10 Democrat to 14–10 Republican in 2020.
- Republicans flipped the New Hampshire House from 230–156 majority Democrat to 213–187 Republican majority in 2020.
- Yet, Joe Biden, who was fourth in the Democrat Party primary in the state, and Kamala Harris, who did not make it to the Democrat primary, won the state 52.7 percent to 45.4 percent to Trump.

In one location in the state, the Rockingham District 7 NH House Race in Windham, New Hampshire, a recount showed that the Dominion-owned voting machines shorted every Republican candidate by roughly 300 votes.

161 (Hoft J. , BIG NEWS FROM NEW HAMPSHIRE! Secretary of State Gardner Agrees to Forensic Audit of Windham's Voting Machines AND Ballots, 2021)

The Dominion-owned machine results were wrong for all four Republicans in Windham by 6 percent or almost exactly 300 votes.[162]

Local citizens petitioned the state to allow a forensic audit of the 2020 results in Rockingham District 77 of both the systems and the ballots. After much discussion, state leaders finally allowed the audit to move forward.[163]

After more discussions and eventual votes, the state leaders in New Hampshire agreed to an audit of the "Windham Incident" in mid-April 2021, five months after the 2020 Election.[164]

The next and most important action to take place in the Windham Incident audit was to pick who would perform the audit. Objective, independent, and competent auditors were required. Unfortunately, New Hampshire picked the wrong auditors to do the job.[165]

On April 27, 2021, it was announced that the Windham Board of Selectmen had chosen the team of Verified Voting to perform the election audit in Windham. That same day, it was discovered that the codirector of Verified Voting, Mark Lindeman, signed and sent a letter in the Maricopa County Audit in Arizona, where he said the election fraud claims there were fake, and he worked to try to get the Maricopa County audit shut down! This guy was going to lead the audit in New Hampshire.[166]

Lindeman joined Liz Howard from the Brennan Center for Justice, and Ryan Macias from RSM Election Technologies in encouraging Arizona Senate leader Karen Fann to end her sanctioned audit in Arizona.[167]

---

162 Ibid

163 Ibid

164 (Hoft J. , BREAKING: New Hampshire Governor SIGNS SB 43 INTO LAW! – Mandates Audit of Windham's Fraudulent 2020 Election Results!, 2021)

165 (Hoft J. , EMERGENCY ALERT: Windham, New Hampshire Officials Choose Far-Left Group to Conduct Forensic Audit — PLEASE CONTACT WINDHAM OFFICIALS TODAY!, 2021)

166 Ibid

167 (Hoft J. , Hey New Hampshire – Look At who 'Verified Voting' (the Firm Selected to Audit Windham) Is Associating With, 2021)

The Brennan Center had a budget of over $84 million in 2020, and its number one donor was George Soros. It was run by Michael Waldman, a former Bill Clinton assistant. RSM Election Technologies was created by Ryan Macias, who was an acting director for a short time at the US Election Assistance Commission (EAC) overseeing the Voting System Testing and Certification Program. Macias was called in to comment on numerous audits after the 2020 Election pushing far-left arguments against these audits. The fact that Lindeman aligned with these organizations and individuals was not a good omen.[168]

Philip Stark, PhD was another auditor selected to perform the audit in New Hampshire. He was an appointee at the federal government's EAC at that time and was appointed by Speaker Nancy Pelosi in 2016.[169] The other auditor selected was Harri Hursti, PhD. As noted in *The Steal - Volume II: The Impossible Occurs*, Hursti presented at the United Nations in 2018 alongside Liz Howard from the Brennan Center to discuss election cybersecurity controls.[170]

The Windham audit went as poorly as expected. Not only was the audit bizarre, but there were conflicts with all the auditors and the Democrat Party. Top Democrats Pelosi and Schumer both had connections with the auditors, which should have disqualified these auditors from participating.[171]

The audit was so poorly done that the audit team looked like they didn't know what they were doing, probably because they didn't. Mark Lindeman of Verified Voting barely showed up and literally stood around with his hands in

---

168 Ibid

169 (Hoft J. , BREAKING EXCLUSIVE: The Windham, New Hampshire 2020 Election Audit Was Over Before It Started – Two of Three Auditors Have Conflicts with Pelosi and Schumer, 2021)

170 (Hoft J. , BREAKING EXCLUSIVE: UN, US, Facebook and Smartmatic Executives Conspired Together Before the 2020 Election and Many of Same Officials Now Trying to Stop or Derail 2020 Election Audits Taking Place, 2021)

171 (Hoft J. , After Missing Several Days and Putting His Hands In His Pockets When He Was Present, Verified Voting's Mark Lindeman Claims The Windham Audit Was 'Robust', 2021)

his pockets when he was present, yet he had the audacity to claim that the audit work in Windham, New Hampshire was "robust."[172]

The second auditor selected to perform the audit, Philip Stark, announced early in the audit that he was leaving, and so the bulk of the work was up to Harri Hursti to complete.[173] Hursti got right down to work. Although the audit was being videotaped, Hursti took off his button-down shirt and began wandering around aimlessly in his white T-shirt. It was the most bizarre scene in US auditing history. When he was done for the day, he put his suit jacket over his T-shirt and never did put his button-down shirt back on.[174]

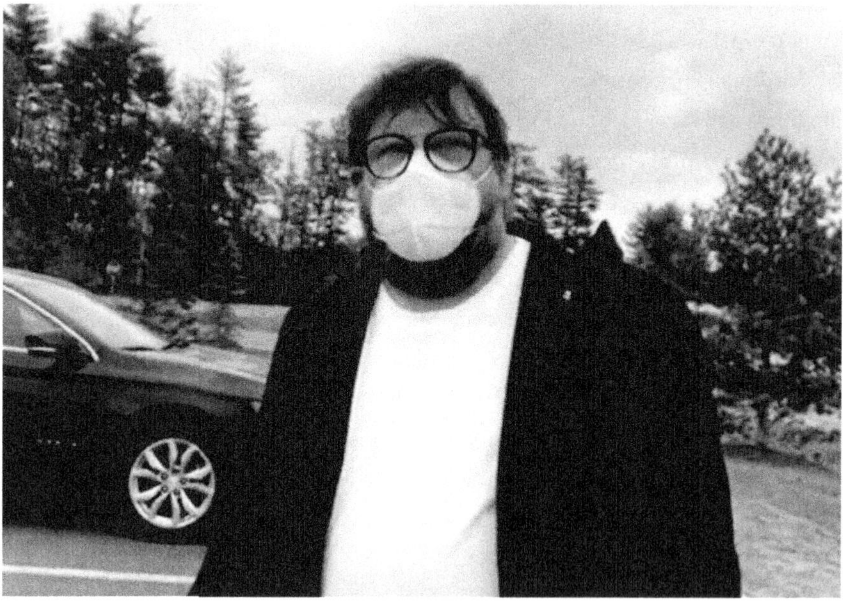

Hursti was famous for his work in 2005, when he uncovered that Diebold memory cards could be easily hacked and manipulated to secretly change vote

172 Ibid

173 (Hoft J. , BREAKING: One of Three Auditors Exits Windham, NH Election Audit – Law Requires a Team of Three Auditors, 2021)

174 (Hoft J. , 'Audit' of Windham, New Hampshire Is a SHAM Due to Conflicts, Independence Issues, and a Ridiculous Audit Program – America Deserves Better, 2021)

counts. He also demonstrated that his hacks were undetectable. His work was so profound that it became known as the "Hursti Hack." However, 15 years later, Hursti agreed to "audit" similar cards, knowing they were likely hackable.[175]

The main issue to be investigated in the Windham audit was why certain ballots in only one machine caused issues. After taking his shirt off and wandering aimlessly Hursti finally concluded that the error was due to "dust." We expected a bogus audit, and we got it.[176]

Maricopa County, Arizona

The people in Arizona knew that their state was stolen in the 2020 Election. The results made no sense. As noted in *The Steal - Volume II: The Impossible Occurs*, Joe Biden, arguably the worst candidate for President in US history, was somehow the first Democrat since Harry Truman to win Maricopa County, Arizona, where Phoenix lies. This, of course, was nonsense, and the people there knew it.

In Maricopa County in Arizona, the largest county in the state, **President Trump set a Republican record for net additional votes by adding roughly 248,000 from his 2016 performance, only to become the first Republican nominee (and incumbent president) to lose the county in 72 years.** This was accomplished by Biden's gain of nearly 338,000 net "new votes" from 2016, which is nearly three times higher than the all-time previous high Democratic vote gain in the county by John Kerry in 2004.[177]

As soon as the results were finalized, the voters in Arizona called for an audit of Maricopa County, the largest county in the state and one of the largest in the country. But any efforts to initiate an audit in the county received panic-driven responses from the Maricopa County Board of Supervisors, who were predominantly self-proclaimed Republicans.

---

175 Op cit, BREAKING EXCLUSIVE…Pelosi and Schumer

176 Op cit, "Audit" of Windham…is a SHAM…

177 (Flynn, 2021)

As time went by, calls for an audit of Maricopa County's 2020 Election results became louder, and efforts to ignore these calls became indefensible. When it reached this point, the Maricopa County Board of Supervisors decided to finally act. They announced that they would allow an audit of the county but only using "accredited" auditors. The county stated that the only firms they would use for the audits were those that were accredited by the EAC. The problem was, as noted in *The Steal - Volume II: The impossible Occurs*, neither audit firm selected was properly accredited at the time of their selection. Once this was reported, the EAC immediately gave these firms their accreditations that day. Ultimately, these firms were selected because they were expected to give a favorable rating of the county's election results in the 2020 Election, something these firms always conclude in all their audits.

The results from the audit firms that performed the audits for the Maricopa County Board of Supervisors ended as expected. The firms performed limited reviews on a sample of machines used in the election. To no one's surprise, they found nothing wrong with the 2020 election results in the County.[178]

At the same time, the Arizona Senate, after listening to their constituents, began efforts to hire auditors to audit the 2020 results in Maricopa County. Liberals went crazy over the news. The local and national media jumped in to do what they could to villainize those who were calling for an audit. Even Hillary's attorney, Marc Elias, who was instrumental in efforts before the 2020 Election to ensure mail-in ballots were in force across the country and especially in swing states, jumped in (see *The Steal - Volume I: Setting the Stage* for more on Marc Elias).

Elias came out and attacked the Senate in a threatening manner. He wasn't the only one.[179] Biden's Attorney General Merrick Garland also threatened the Arizona Senate in June 2021 with an announcement that the DOJ would

---

178 (Hoft J. , Maricopa County Audits Are Proving to Be a Waste of Time and Money, They Were Never Created to Identify the Suspected Election Fraud in the County, 2021)

179 (Hoft J. , Democrats in Arizona Are Petrified – They're Bringing in Marc Elias's Perkins Coie to Make Threats and Make the Maricopa County Audit Go Away, 2021)

scrutinize the post-election audits for evidence of voting law violations. Arizona Senator Wendy Rogers responded to Garland's threat with a simple message:[180]

> You will not touch Arizona ballots or machines unless you want to spend time in an Arizona prison. Maybe you should focus on stopping terrorism. The Justice Department is one of the most corrupt institutions in the USA.

None of the efforts by the corrupt left and RINOs in Maricopa County stopped the Arizona Senate from moving forward with the audit. After months of attempting to obtain access to the ballots, the Senate finally won a court case, where the judge ordered the ballots in the county to be provided to the Senate.[181]

In response to the court's ruling and before being told when and where to deliver the ballots to the Senate, the Maricopa County Board of Supervisors loaded the ballots onto a truck. It is believed that this move of the ballots was not performed under the proper chain of custody. It is also unknown where the truck went with the ballots. The ballots were eventually unloaded back into the county's warehouse where the same ballots presumably came from and placed back in the County's custody. Note that it's impossible to know where these ballots went and who oversaw their move without proper chain of custody. **Without the proper chain of custody, this act alone invalidated any audit of the Maricopa County ballots related to the 2020 Election**.[182]

A few days after this episode, with the ballots being trucked to God knows where, it was reported that shredded 2020 Election ballots were found in a dumpster outside the building where the ballots were kept. Later that same day, a fire was reported at one of the Board of Supervisor's properties. Clint Hickman's Hickman Farms suffered the loss of two chicken barns and 165,000

---

180 (Hoft J. , Arizona Lawmaker Responds to AG Garland: "You Will Not Touch Arizona Ballots or Machines Unless You Want to Spend Time in Arizona Prison", 2021)

181 (Hoft J. , After Finding Shredded Ballots in the Dumpster Earlier Today – A Mysterious Fire Breaks Out at Maricopa County Official's Farm, 2021)

182 Ibid

chickens due to a fire at the property about an hour west of Phoenix that same day.[183]

Some readers of the reports of the Hickman fire in Arizona thought that maybe there was some shred that burned along with the severely blackened chickens.

The audit did finally get underway on April 22, 2021, with all the ballots and machines delivered to the Maricopa County Veterans Memorial Coliseum in Phoenix. There was great hope as the nation was watching to see if the audit would uncover any material issues in the certified results in the county.

Months later, after the audit was finished, we learned that the audit should have ended within three days of it starting. A report from the floor of the audit where the initial counting of ballots took place claimed that in the first three days of the audit, every box examined by the team was not properly sealed. Not one box on the first 13 out of roughly 44 pallets of ballots (roughly 25 percent of all the ballots) was properly sealed. This should have ended the ballot review portion of the audit then and there, because none of these ballots were secured properly. Any one of the ballots could have been tampered with during the election or since. But the audit wasn't stopped; it moved on as if nothing was wrong.[184]

Former Arizona GOP Secretary of State, Ken Bennett, who was involved in the audit shared at that time to a local reporter from *The Gateway Pundit*, Jordan Conradson:[185]

> Well, we still don't have the chain of custody documents that the county must have kept between when the ballots were put in the warehouse after the November election to when they were delivered to us on April 22nd. We know that one of the county officials tweeted out a photo of some of the ballot pallets being loaded into the back of a truck as though they were ready to deliver them to the Senate.

---

183 Ibid

184 (Hoft J. , BREAKING EXCLUSIVE: The 2021 Maricopa Audit Proved After Three Days that the 2020 Election in Arizona Was Uncertifiable (Part I), 2022)

185 Ibid

> And so we would like to see if their chain of custody documents between November and April include movement of the ballots like that. We have complete chain of custody from the day that they brought the ballots to us, while we've been holding the ballots. But we're still looking for the chain of custody documentation between the election and April.

This issue was noted in a letter sent to Maricopa County officials in May, 2021, from the Arizona Senate and signed by GOP Senate Majority leader Karen Fann. In this letter, the following was noted:[186]

> As the audit has progressed, the Senate's contractors have become aware of apparent omissions, inconsistencies, and anomalies relating to Maricopa County's handling, organization, and storage of ballots. We hope you can assist us in understanding these issues, including specifically the following:
>
> 1. The County has not provided any chain-of-custody documentation for the ballots. Does such documentation exist, and if so, will it be produced?
> 2. The bags in which the ballots were stored are not sealed, although the audit team has found at the bottom of many boxes cut seals of the type that would have sealed a ballot bag. Why were these seals placed at the bottom of the boxes?
> 3. Batches within a box are frequently separated by only a divider without any indication of the corresponding batch numbers. In some cases, the batch dividers are missing altogether. This lack of organization has significantly complicated and delayed the audit team's ballot processing efforts. What are the County's procedures for sorting, organizing, and packaging ballot batches?

186 (Hoft J. , BREAKING EXCLUSIVE: The 2021 Maricopa Audit Was a Crime Scene After 3 Days When Every Seal on Every Box Was Found Broken Before Review (Part II), 2022)

4. Most of the ballot boxes were sealed merely with regular tape and not secured by any kind of tamper-evident seal. Is that the County's customary practice for storing ballots?
5. The audit team has encountered a significant number of instances in which there is a disparity between the actual number of ballots contained in a batch and the total denoted on the pink report slip accompanying the batch. In most of these instances, the total on the pink report slip is greater than the number of ballots in the batch, although there are a few instances in which the total is lower. What are the reasons for these discrepancies?

In the final report from the auditors, this issue was not highlighted, but the report did state: "Paper ballots are the best evidence of voter intent, and there is no reliable evidence that the paper ballots were altered to any material degree."

This totally discounted the seriousness of this issue. There was no evidence that the ballots were secure and not tampered with, because of the lack of chain of custody on these ballots, bags not sealed, boxes not sealed, and the many disparities between the actual number of ballots present and the number of ballots reported to be in the ballot boxes. The audit should have ended long before this point, because the results were not certifiable with this material deficiency enveloping the ballots provided for review.[187]

Nevertheless, numerous issues were identified in the audit of Maricopa County, but you wouldn't know it from the final presentations to the Arizona Senate. There was no overall summary at the beginning of the presentation highlighting the material issues similar to what would be done in any audit committee meeting in any Fortune 500 corporation. Rather than summarizing the total number of issues identified in the audit, the presentations from multiple individuals lasted for three hours or more, and the overall results were difficult to gather.

187 Ibid

The results of the ballot review were extensive and by themselves proved the results in Maricopa County in 2020 never should have been certified for Joe Biden. Despite not performing signature reviews, which would have likely involved tens of thousands of additional issues, there still were hundreds of thousands of ballot issues identified in the Maricopa County audit.[188]

The results of the ballot work performed in the audit identified over 428,000 ballot issues identified and listed in the auditors' presentation:

1. The biggest issue identified in the audit was over **255,000** ballots that were early votes counted in the election with no record of being received in the early voting file. Where did they come from?
2. The second-largest issue noted in the Cyber Ninja report included **86,000** ballots where the insureds had no related fingerprints at all, which in this day and age seems unlikely. For these voters, either their name was not found in a regional database, or their last name was not found on the database at the address they were recorded as living in when they were registered to vote. We don't know if these voters were even real people.
3. Cyber Ninjas also listed more than **57,000** issues with ballots in multiple other areas of focus that they audited.
4. Dr. Shiva Ayyadurai presented at the Senate hearing and discussed his work related to the mail-in ballot envelopes where over **29,000** discrepancies were identified. He reported 17,000 ballot envelopes that were duplicates and another 9,500 ballot envelopes that were missing where Maricopa County claimed they were received. In addition, there were over 2,500 issues with signatures, even though a signature check was not included in the scope of the audit. Also, the audit had no chain of custody review for the required documentation.

---

188 (Hoft J. , BREAKING: THE LIST – Nearly 700,000 Maricopa County Ballots Identified with Issues from the Audit and Separate Canvassing Work to Date, 2021)

The results of the audit work performed by IT auditors were enough to decertify the election in Arizona as well. Below are some items on that list:[189]

1. What Maricopa County **has told** the public is often drastically different than their response to the legal subpoena.
2. **Maricopa didn't use** a forensically secure process to clone drives. Dates and times were altered by their cloning process.
3. On March 11, 2021, someone with "Admin access" to the election management system (EMS) **ran a script** that produced 37,646 queries looking for blank passwords. The system has only eight user accounts.
4. Windows Security Event Logs before February 5, 2021, were missing.
5. Every election Administrator account, no matter the user, all had the **same password**.
6. When the Dominion software was installed in August 2019, Administrative passwords were created and haven't been changed since.
7. **The vulnerabilities** that exist on the Maricopa election systems would take an average **script kiddie** less than 10 minutes to gain access to these systems.
8. Maricopa's election system uses iButton key fobs as the second step in logins. Maricopa and Dominion have refused to provide these fobs to auditors.
9. **It's become readily** apparent there are severe cybersecurity problems with the way the election management system and network was maintained.
10. After both sides agreed on a solution, Maricopa County then **refused to release that router data**.
11. Maricopa can't check the configuration of its own election system without relying on Dominion employees.

189 (Hoft J. , Cyber Ninjas Found So Many Issues with the Voting Machines and Processes in Maricopa County It's a Wonder the Previous Auditors Didn't Find These Issues Too, 2021)

12. The two EAC audits hired by Maricopa didn't appear to have addressed cybersecurity aspects, not even shared passwords.
13. **Not a single bit of data** was changed on any device in the auditor's possession. Use of a "write block" device prevented this. Images were made bit by bit, then an MD5 hash value was applied. **There is no need to purchase new machines.**
14. There were no antivirus updates, operating system updates, or security patches applied to the election system since August 2019, the date Dominion software was installed.

Due to the manner in which the results of the audit work were presented, it was difficult to determine what the results of the Maricopa audit were. The media reports as a result of the audit presentation were that Biden gained votes in the counting of the ballots. Due to chain-of-custody issues, this exercise shouldn't even have been performed because the result was tainted. This, however, was the talking point used by the media to discredit the audit, those who worked there, and those who volunteered their own time to make sure the results in Maricopa County in 2020 were accurate.

This audit showed unequivocally that the 2020 election results in Arizona never should have been certified. However, after the audit was finished, nothing happened. The Arizona Senate never voted on decertifying the election, and the crimes identified during the audit were ignored.

New Mexico

Another audit of the 2020 Election was performed in New Mexico. Professor and attorney David Clements, his wife Erin Clements with an engineering background, and a group of local citizens got together to investigate the election results in a couple of counties in the state. Attorney Clements was an award-winning professor who really enjoyed his dream job in New Mexico as a professor. He was terminated after the 2020 Election after he started looking into the 2020 Election fraud.

This audit group was attacked by the New Mexico Secretary of State when they dared to perform the audit. Erin Clements shared in an interview:[190]

> Well, the County Commission obviously should have the power to look at them, because they have to certify the results of the elections . . . But the County Commission got a threat, one of many threatening letters from the Secretary of State's office, saying that if you touch anything, we're going to decommission them and make you buy new ones.

Not only did the state attack these auditors, but the US House of Representatives did as well. Yahoo reported in early 2020:

> The House Oversight Committee is launching an investigation into a partisan ballot review in Otero County, New Mexico, where a self-proclaimed "audit force" is going door to door and questioning voters.
>
> The county, which borders Texas and has about 67,000 residents, agreed this year to pay nearly $50,000 to EchoMail, one of the subcontractors involved in Arizona's partisan ballot review, to review its 2020 election results.
>
> "The Committee is investigating whether your company's audit and canvass in New Mexico illegally interferes with Americans' right to vote by spreading disinformation about elections and intimidating voters," House Oversight Committee Chairwoman Carolyn Maloney, D-NY, and Jamie Raskin, D-Md, the chairman of the subcommittee on civil rights and civil liberties, wrote in a Wednesday letter addressed to VA Shiva Ayyadurai, the founder of EchoMail.

Dr. Shiva stepped away from the audit at around this time, and the auditors in the state reached out to Jeff Lenberg to complete the IT work in the audit. Lenberg had done IT work in the Michigan and Maricopa audits.

---

190 (Hoft J. , Democrats and Dominion Now Trying to Stop 2020 Election Audit in New Mexico – US House Oversight Committee Getting Involved, 2022)

There were numerous challenges and attacks that this audit group endured, but when they were finished, they were happy with their work and believed they performed a thorough review. The audit team ended up performing partial audits in eight counties in New Mexico and a forensic audit in one county, Otero County.[191]

One item the IT audit group found when the audit results were discussed was that the **voting machines used in the state had the ability to fill in ballots**. This was something that also confirmed in an audit in New York in 2019.[192]

In addition, when presenting the results of the IT review, Lenberg shared the following:[193]

1. **Election security is almost nonexistent**. "The systems and the processes that exist are like Swiss cheese."
2. Pro V&V [one of the audit firms used by Maricopa County, noted above] certifies voting machines across the country but does not do a good job. They don't have the resources to.
3. Wherever they went they received full-fledged resistance when wanting to look at the voting systems.
4. **Risk-limiting audits are a facade** in the way they're being done.
5. The **password** for Michigan and New Mexico voting system access was **"123456"**, and you can access all the administrative menus with this password. You can go in days after an election and add ballots and adjust the time and print it out. This capability should not exist in the system.

191 (Hoft J. , Attorney David Clements Discusses the 2020 Election Work in New Mexico "Focusing More on the Machine-Driven Aspects of Fraud", 2022)

192 (Hoft J. , SHOCKING: Per New Mexico Auditors Dominion Voting Systems Can Fill-In Ballots – Uncovered 2019 New York State Audit Confirms This, 2022)

193 (Hoft J. , BOMBSHELL: Evidence Shows Michigan Supreme Court Race in 2020 Was Flipped – Election Audit Professionals Also Identify Numerous Red Flags in New Mexico and Arizona, 2022)

6. Microsoft **SQL software was found** in Michigan, New Mexico, and Arizona. It does not need to be there. It can be accessed without any password, and you have "keys to the kingdom." You can do anything you want with the data and change anything you want with SQL.
7. Transparency is necessary where everything is recorded. The only place ballots can be associated with voters is at the polling place.
8. In Maricopa County, Arizona, all the ballot boxes were unsealed when they were provided to the auditors.
9. In Maricopa County, there were 263,000 corrupted images that were also not mentioned by the auditors there (Biden was given the win by 10,000 votes).
10. There were 21,000 ballot images missing in Maricopa.
11. In New Mexico, they updated the software that was certified, which makes no sense, and in the process **deleted the 2020 project file**.
12. There was a pile of red flags from the system audit work.

The canvassing work in this audit identified patterns in the voter rolls that should not be there. Across the state, when looking at only a few months of data at a time and when splitting registrations out by party, **a clear, repeating weekly pattern emerges in the voter rolls** where the independent voters magically track with the GOP, and the Democrats always manage to out-register the GOP by approximately the same percentage every day, and this has been going on for years.[194]

SUMMARY

US corporations are required to ensure their financials are accurate, and the processes involved in aggregating their financial related data are well controlled. They do this by hiring independent and objective auditors to perform audits to determine that the financials are accurate, and the processes and

194 (Hoft J. , EXCLUSIVE FINDING: Patterns Identified in New Mexico Voter Rolls Are Not Consistent with Random, Human Behavior – What's Going On?, 2022)

systems involved in accumulating these financials are all working as intended. The processes should be reliable, consistent, and accurate, and the IT systems should be functioning properly and securely.

These same quality audits are not performed in the US elections.

If systems were not made available to auditors in corporate audits of US companies, the auditors would never give the related corporation a positive or non-qualified audit opinion. Yet, this is what was done after the 2020 Election.

Perhaps the most obvious shortcoming in the 2020 Election was the effort after the election to prevent audits from being performed. Without independent, objective, and transparent audits embedded in the 2020 Election in key swing states, the results of the election should never have been certified.

7

Hunter Biden's Laptop

John Paul Mac Isaac had a computer repair shop in Delaware. His life was turned upside down a couple of years ago when about 10 minutes before closing on Friday evening, April 12, 2019, Hunter Biden stumbled into his shop.[195]

John Paul Mac Isaac

Mac Isaac said that he didn't know who Hunter Biden was at first. He also commented that Hunter was a bit out of sorts; he could smell the alcohol on his breath. That evening, Hunter brought in three MacBook Pro laptops with him, and all were water damaged. The first laptop that Mac Isaac looked at was water damaged beyond repair. He handed that back to Hunter.[196]

The second laptop needed a keyboard to work. Mac Isaac handed a portable keyboard to Hunter and noted that to this day, Hunter never paid him for it.[197]

---

195 (Hoft J. , "On that Drive, There Was More than Enough Evidence of Wrongdoing in the Ukraine Under the Previous [Obama] Administration" – Exclusive with John Paul Mac Isaac – Computer Repairman Who Handled Hunter Biden's Laptop, 2022)

196 Ibid

197 Ibid

Mac Isaac agreed to copy the third laptop to a flash drive if he was able to. Mac Isaac filled out a work order and had Hunter sign it. It included standard language that if Hunter didn't come back to collect the laptop, it would become Mac Isaac's property.[198]

The third laptop had problems with its power where it would shut off periodically. Because of this, it took Mac Isaac some time to download the data from that machine. Mac Isaac could only copy small amounts of data at a time because he risked the laptop shutting down. During this download process, Mac Isaac noticed lots of porn and lots of financial information housed on the laptop.[199]

Mac Isaac completed his task, but even after repeated calls, Hunter never came back for the laptop. At about that same time, it was reported that Hunter's father, Joe Biden, was running for office. Mac Isaac found himself, a computer repairman in Delaware, sitting on the laptop and a copy of the laptop with all sorts of potentially politically damaging information on it. This was in his possession, and Hunter's dad just announced he was running for President for the third time.[200]

Mac Isaac was desperately trying to get the laptop out of his shop. This thing was like housing a hornets' nest in his store. He wanted it out. Eventually, he contacted his father who lived in Arizona, and his father, a former military guy, offered to bring a copy of the laptop to the FBI in Arizona. Unfortunately, the FBI had no interest in what Mac Isaac's father had to say.[201]

Sometime later, Mac Isaac received a visit from the FBI at his store. They took Hunter's laptop with them. He knew based on their actions that they were never going to do a thing with it. This was now in late 2019, and the first bogus impeachment of President Trump was taking place within the corrupt House of Representatives led by Nancy Pelosi. The impeachment was related to Biden's activities in Ukraine. Mac Isaac knew there was plenty of information related to Hunter Biden on Ukraine on that laptop.

---

198 Ibid

199 Ibid

200 Ibid

201 Ibid

"What I had seen on that drive, there was more than enough evidence of wrongdoing in the Ukraine under the previous [Obama] Administration." The impeachment challenged President Trump's interest in Biden's actions in Ukraine, claiming in essence that he never should have addressed this topic.[202]

Mac Isaac shared that when the FBI departed an agent gave him a warning like a mafia hitman might do.

> "Nothing ever happens to people who don't talk about these kind of things." I saw that as a thinly veiled threat, so I made zero effort to talk to the FBI after that point. I did get a phone call from that same agent about two weeks later before Christmas, asking if anybody had come in representing Hunter requesting the equipment. And he seemed actually kinda surprised, so by this time, I was nervous that the FBI's agenda no longer [was] concerned with my safety and concerned about getting that laptop back to the previous owner.
>
> Obviously, when that impeachment trial happened and that laptop was no longer to be seen, I knew I was in trouble, because if the FBI wasn't going to submit that as evidence, then it's probably at the bottom of the river. What does that mean? What's going to happen to me?

Mac Isaac was cautious, and because of this, he kept a couple of copies of Hunter's laptop. Eventually, Mac Isaac was able to get one copy to Rudi Giuliani, President Trump's attorney. Mac Isaac shared:[203]

> I figured my days were numbered, so I stepped out of the shadows, and I traded my fear for courage, and I reached out to Rudy Giuliani's office . . .

That's when things got moving, slowly at first. The FBI never did provide any information from Hunter's laptop to the Democrat-led bogus impeachment

---

202 Ibid

203 Ibid

hearing of President Trump. They had the information to indict Hunter on numerous crimes and validate President Trump's effort to uncover the Bidens' criminal actions in Ukraine on the laptop, but instead, the FBI hid the laptop from the public.

The Trump impeachment hearing was one of the most corrupt actions ever taken in the US House. This all could have been averted had the FBI been honest and done its job. Instead, the FBI lied by omission and withheld material evidence on the Hunter Biden laptop that would have exonerated President Trump of any wrongdoing while providing ample evidence of corruption by the Biden gang in Ukraine.

While that was going on, there were efforts to pass the information and details showing crimes and corruption from Hunter's laptop to the media. No one would touch the topic. It was like a hot potato, and no one wanted it. Then in October 2020, about a month before the 2020 Election, the *New York Post* released some articles regarding what was in Hunter Biden's laptop.

The Laptop Revealed

On Wednesday, October 14, 2020, the *New York Post* released an article about information found on Hunter's laptop. Rudy Giuliani had reportedly shared a copy of the laptop—or portions of the copy of the laptop—with *The Post*, which started as follows:[204]

> Hunter Biden introduced his father, then-Vice President Joe Biden, to a top executive at a Ukrainian energy firm less than a year before the elder Biden pressured government officials in Ukraine into firing a prosecutor who was investigating the company, according to emails obtained by *The Post*.
>
> The never-before-revealed meeting is mentioned in a message of appreciation that Vadym Pozharskyi, an adviser to the board of Burisma, allegedly sent Hunter Biden on April 17, 2015, about a year

204 (Fonrouge, 2020)

> after Hunter joined the Burisma board at a reported salary of up to $50,000 a month.
>
> "Dear Hunter, thank you for inviting me to DC and giving an opportunity to meet your father and spent [sic] some time together. It's realty [sic] an honor and pleasure," the email reads.
>
> An earlier email from May 2014 also shows Pozharskyi, reportedly Burisma's No. 3 exec, asking Hunter for "advice on how you could use your influence" on the company's behalf.
>
> The blockbuster correspondence—which flies in the face of Joe Biden's claim that he's "never spoken to my son about his overseas business dealings"—is contained in a massive trove of data recovered from a laptop computer.

According to *The Post*, Steve Bannon told *The Post* about the existence of the laptop and Rudy Giuliani provided a copy of the laptop. This was the first we heard of Hunter's laptop.[205]

Big Media Response

The New York Times wrote a piece about the *New York Post's* reporting. *The Times* claimed that *The Post's* reporters themselves questioned the credibility of the article.[206]

Newsweek was even quicker to address *The Post's* report in an article the following day:[207]

> The *New York Post* on Wednesday published an article claiming to report emails between Democratic presidential nominee Joe Biden's son Hunter Biden and a Ukrainian business associate thanking the

205 Ibid

206 (Robertson, 2020)

207 (Lemon, 2020)

> former vice president's son for arranging a meeting with his father in April 2015, and urging him to use his "influence" in May 2014.
>
> Facebook and Twitter moved quickly to restrict the reach of the *Post* article on Wednesday. Facebook said it was restricting the article's reach until it could undergo a rigorous fact-checking process. Twitter cited its policies about hacked material and doxing to justify its decision to limit the article's spread, blocking links to the article and images from the report from being shared. Meanwhile, both the authenticity and accuracy of the article remained in question.
>
> President Donald Trump and his allies have long pushed a narrative that Joe Biden acted corruptly during his time as vice president to benefit his son Hunter's business interests in Ukraine and China. Although former State Department officials have testified before Congress that Biden's son's business dealings in the foreign countries raised concerns about potential conflicts of interest, no substantive evidence has come forward to confirm claims that Biden acted corruptly. Even a detailed 87-page report on the concerns released by Senate Republicans in September did not demonstrate that the Democratic candidate or his son had acted in an illegal or unethical manner.

Newsweek went on to support the former Vice President and suggest that his actions may not even be illegal. The debate was on about Hunter's laptop and what was reportedly in it.[208]

CNN also came out with a hit-piece on the existence of Hunter's laptop, that Sunday, October 18:[209]

> *CNN* hasn't been able to authenticate emails, and the *New York Post* declined to comment.

208 Ibid

209 (Benveniste, 2020)

> "This is a classic example of the right-wing media machine," [*CNN*'s Chief Media Correspondent Brian] Stelter said. "*FOX* and Trump have this in common: They want you to stay mad and stay tuned."
>
> The story is a "manufactured scandal," Stelter said, meant to feed "whataboutism"—an opportunity for the right-wing media to shift the conversation from Trump's record to Biden's.
>
> "The strategy is to deflect attention, to attack the opponent, and the same propaganda pipeline is there all the time," said Yochai Benkler, a professor at Harvard Law School [who] told Stelter on "Reliable Sources" Sunday.
>
> Benkler noted that when Hillary Clinton's emails, and the FBI investigation into her handling of classified information that ultimately recommended no charges, and the Clinton foundation became the subject of right-wing media talking points, serious journalists dug into her emails.
>
> "I think this time, unlike what we saw with Clinton, where serious journalists fell for the Bannon-produced Clinton Foundation nonsense trivially, where serious journalists dug into the emails, and Gallup shows us, the only thing people thought about when they thought about Clinton was emails and foundation," Benkler said.
>
> Right-wing media is trying for the same strategy again as Election Day grows closer.
>
> But unlike previous "closing argument" stories, the media world has largely ignored *The Post's* Hunter Biden story.
>
> "They're so confident that the story's just going to be too much fun for serious journalists not to pick up," Benkler said. "They're trying to produce it now, but the media at the moment – major professional media – doesn't seem to be falling for it."

CNN was right about one thing: Big Media and Big Tech were doing their best to cover-up the story from *The Post*. Like four years earlier, when the Hillary Clinton and Podesta emails released by Wikileaks, media giants and Big Tech were not going to discuss or promote the emails found on Hunter Biden's laptop.

Russia Propaganda Claims

On October 19, 2020, a group of more than 50 Deep State actors released a statement saying that the Hunter Biden laptop reports were Russian disinformation. This was reported by far-left *Politico*.[210]

> More than 50 former senior intelligence officials have signed on to a letter outlining their belief that the recent disclosure of emails allegedly belonging to Joe Biden's son "has all the classic earmarks of a Russian information operation."
>
> The letter, signed on Monday, centers around a batch of documents released by the *New York Post* last week that purport to tie the Democratic nominee to his son Hunter's business dealings. Under the banner headline "Biden Secret E-mails," *The Post* reported it was given a copy of Hunter Biden's laptop hard drive by President Donald Trump's personal lawyer Rudy Giuliani, who said he got it from a Mac shop owner in Delaware who also alerted the FBI.
>
> While the letter's signatories presented no new evidence, they said their national security experience had made them "deeply suspicious that the Russian government played a significant role in this case" and cited several elements of the story that suggested the Kremlin's hand at work.
>
> "If we are right," they added, "this is Russia trying to influence how Americans vote in this election, and we believe strongly that Americans need to be aware of this."
>
> Nick Shapiro, a former top aide under CIA director John Brennan, provided *Politico* with the letter on Monday. He noted that "the IC leaders who have signed this letter worked for the past four presidents, including Trump. The real power here however is the number of former, working-level IC officers who want the American people to know that once again the Russians are interfering."

---

210 (Bertrand, 2020)

After multiple incidents of being played by the Deep State, you'd have to wonder how anyone could visit Big Media sites and expect to be told the truth?

This story was aired all over Big Media. The Deep State wanted to make sure that Americans heard that the Hunter laptop was a forgery. This, of course, was not the truth.

At this same time, President Trump's Director of National Intelligence, John Ratcliff, blasted Adam Schiff and others who were claiming the laptop was part of some Russian disinformation campaign. Ratcliff stated that this was not the truth. Individuals like former Obama lackeys John Brennan, and James Clapper were on the list of Deep State signors. Ratcliff was speaking the truth.[211]

Laptop Confirmed

Less than a year later, *Politico* backtracked and confirmed that some of the stories shared by the *New York Post* before the 2020 Election were real.

> *Politico Playbook* published reporting from correspondent Ben Schreckinger's new book, *The Bidens*, which delved into the emails that surfaced in the explosive reporting that was ultimately suppressed by Big Tech.
>
> "A person who had independent access to Hunter Biden's emails confirmed he did receive a 2015 email from a Ukrainian businessman thanking him for the chance to meet Joe Biden. The same goes for a 2017 email in which a proposed equity breakdown of a venture with Chinese energy executives includes the line, '10 held by H for the big guy?'" the *Playbook* wrote.
>
> "Emails released by a Swedish government agency also match emails in the leaked cache, and two people who corresponded with Hunter Biden confirmed emails from the cache were genuine."

211 (Hoft J. , 50 Former Intel Officials Including Clapper and Brennan Sign Letter Saying Hunter Biden Emails Story is Russian Disinformation — Despite DNI Ratcliffe's Statement, 2020)

When far-left *Politico* confirms it's wrong, that is a big deal. The 50-plus former intel officers were left in shame. Their words no longer can be trusted. Former Obama DNI James Clapper, former Obama CIA Director John Brennan, Former CIA Director Mike Hayden, former CIA Director Leon Panetta, and many more added their names to the wall of shame, all in the name of corrupt and senile Joe Biden.[212]

In late April of 2023, the US House Judiciary Committee revealed a shocking development based on testimony by Michael Morell, a former Deputy Director of the Central Intelligence Agency (CIA) and one of the 50+ signatories of the letter stating that he Hunter Biden laptop story was Russia disinformation. Morell revealed that US Secretary of State Antony Blinken, then senior adviser to the Biden campaign, was the impetus of the public statement signed in October 2020 that falsely implied the *New York Post*'s reporting about Hunter Biden was the product of Russian disinformation. It was all a lie, and Biden's Secretary of State Blinken was behind it.[213]

THE PERVERSE BIDEN FAMILY

A significant piece of information that to this day has been mostly ignored by the media related to the Hunter Biden laptop is the sick and seedy pictures, videos, and text messages found on the laptop. While the media and Big Tech were trying to downplay the financial information on the laptop concerning bribes and other Biden corrupt international dealings, the behind-the-scenes realities of Hunter Biden, his perversions, and his family's responses found on the laptop were being ignored.

Two weeks before the 2020 Election XRVision provided me actionable intelligence to publish at The Gateway Pundit regarding Hunter Biden and his network's financial fraud, national security breaches, and criminal conduct. At this time there wasn't enough time to go through all the financial related data on the laptop. Because of this, the corrupt, drug addicted activities saved on the laptop were uncovered and presented to the

212 (Johnson, 2021)

213 (Committee, 2023)

public. The world needed to know how perverse the Biden family was that was running for the office of President of the United States.

On the morning of October 26, 2020, less than ten days before the 2020 Election, the first article in a series of articles was released on Hunter Biden at *The Gateway Pundit*. In this article, a series of text messages that Hunter had backed up onto his laptop were provided that showed that Joe Biden and Jill Biden were aware of Hunter's actions with a certain minor. Joe and Jill set a rule with Hunter where he couldn't be in the same room with the minor without another adult in the room.[214]

After the first article in the series received a lot of attention, the next day came the second article in the series. On Tuesday, October 27, 2020, an article showing Hunter's connections with Russians with the potential for blackmail were released. Hunter had saved photos of his activities on his laptop. For years, we heard the left claimed Russia was holding blackmail information on Donald Trump. This was a complete lie. It was all made up. But after uncovering photos of Hunter at a luxurious property in West Hollywood naked and involved in what appeared to be an orgy, the Russians certainly had blackmail tapes on Hunter Biden to use against a Biden administration.[215]

On Wednesday, less than a week before the 2020 election, *The Gateway Pundit* released another article on Hunter Biden from pictures obtained on his laptop. Hunter held inappropriate pictures of a minor on his laptop. The text messages from a few days prior were revisited along with the pictures.[216]

On Day 4 of the series, another truth bomb from the laptop was unearthed. Hunter Biden maintained a Pornhub account where he loaded pictures of a

---

214 (Hoft J. , BREAKING EXCLUSIVE: Text Messages Show VP Biden and His Wife Colluded to Suppress HUNTER'S ACTIONS WITH A CERTAIN MINOR, 2020)

215 (Hoft J. , BREAKING EXCLUSIVE: Hunter Biden's "RUSSIAN BLACKMAIL PHOTOS" Uncovered – Hunter with Russians in Hollywood, 2020)

216 (Hoft J. , BREAKING EXCLUSIVE: Hunter Biden Held Inappropriate Pictures of Certain Minor — Joe Biden Is Lying, 2020)

family member. Pictures from the account were also on his laptop. Hunter shared these pornographic pictures for the whole world to see.[217]

The entire picture of the Biden family and of Hunter Biden was a mess. Hunter was a drug addict with all the money he needed, all the drugs he wanted, and all the protection from the federal government that he could ask for. This entire scenario depicted Hunter as an animal and the family floundering trying to keep Hunter's actions out of the press. This was the family that was vying for the Presidency, and America had a right to know who and what they were putting in the White House.

This was only the beginning of reporting on the Hunter Biden laptop. There was much more to report. One observation was that the same things that the Deep State accused Carter Page of were things Hunter Biden actually was participating in.[218]

The Steele dossier accused Carter Page of being involved with an energy company in Russia and of President Trump hooking up with Russian hookers overseas. Hunter was involved with Chinese energy company CEFC, and he was involved with Russian women in West Hollywood.[219]

Hunter's relationship with CEFC was more than just another deal between the Vice President's son and China. It was a deal between Hunter and the head of CEFC, who Hunter labeled the "richest man in the world," who disappeared a short time later, never to be found. Hunter also initiated the deal with CEFC with Chinese spy chief, Patrick Ho.[220]

For the Bidens, it was all about the money. In 2013, Hunter Biden joined his father, then Vice President Joe Biden on an official government trip to China. It was during this trip that Hunter—inexperienced and out of place—was able to secure $1.5 billion from China for a private equity fund that he was forming

---

217 (Hoft J. , HUGE BREAKING EXCLUSIVE: Hunter Biden Has a PornHub Account Where He Uploaded His Personal Porn – Including with Family Member, 2020)

218 (Hoft J. , EXCLUSIVE: Carter Page Was Accused of Doing with Russia Exactly What Hunter Biden Did with China, 2020)

219 Ibid

220 (Laila, BREAKING: Hunter Biden Audio Confesses Partnership with China 'Spy Chief' — Joe Biden Named as Witness in SDNY Criminal Case #LaptopFromHell, 2020)

at the time. In 2015, Hunter's Bohai Harvest joined forces with the Chinese military contractor, Aviation Industry Corporation of China (AVIC), to buy American parts manufacturer Henniges Automotive. AVIC was identified as a front group for China's military and was notorious for stealing US military technology to build China's own fighter jets and drones.[221]

For the Biden family, the business of politics was the business of taking what they could from whoever they could. They were the fixers for those in need and the targets for foreign nations. Hunter's drug addiction magnified the corruption and brought out the worst in the already corrupt and seedy family. There was no way the Deep State was going to let the evidence of the Bidens' crimes and corruption make the light of day in the US before the election. Some believe Joe Biden never would have won the election if the American people knew the truth about Hunter and Joe Biden. Clearly, it would have made the steal much more difficult had America been told the truth.

221 (Hoft J. , DAY 2 BOMBSHELL: Newly Released Emails Show How Hunter Biden Worked to Cash in Big on China WITH MONEY HELD FOR HIS DAD, JOE BIDEN!, 2020)

8

The Censorship Complex

Big Media and Big Tech were involved in Big-Time Collusion before, during, and after the 2020 Election.

We knew that Big Media and Big Tech were behind the Democrats and were happily ignoring any of their America-killing corrupt policies. We also knew that the Deep State was involved in the rolling coup of President Trump with the constant Russia, Russia, Russia lie. But we never knew how much they were working with each other until 2022.

In the first book in this series, *The Steal - Volume I: Setting the Stage*, both the Big Media and Big Tech were covered in separate chapters. The steal could not have occurred without the mainstream media and social media totally in the corner for Joe Biden. We never knew how much this was the case. **Two years later, information would come out that would shock even those of us who knew the media and Big Tech were in Biden's pocket.**

Big Media

In *The Steal - Volume I: Setting the Stage*, one chapter was dedicated to the corrupt and biased actions of American media. We saw how biased the media had become during the George W. Bush years. The media was horrible and attacked Bush daily and relentlessly. The left-wing media threw many hit pieces at President Bush, and unfortunately, he had no answers.

Then came along Obama, and he could literally do no wrong in the eyes of this media. Despite policies that ignored the common man and the financial challenges related to the Great Recession, Obama was praised. The wars continued and more wars were started. Obama and Hillary moved guns into Libya, which helped the anti-America terrorists take over that nation and murder Gaddafi. The same guns were then moved to Syria out of Benghazi, and the media remained silent. The guns landed in the hands of the rebels who morphed into ISIS, and the media remained silent.[222] Obama sent millions to Iran, and the media remained silent.

Americans could see what Obama was doing to the country inside and out, but not the media. Obamacare was a socialist takeover of the healthcare system that instituted government mandates on medical decisions. The media said nothing.

This led to President Trump. He saw right through the media. He learned right away that the media was not honest when it came to his campaign. Americans knew it too and were happy to finally have a political candidate who stood up to the media and called them what they were: "fake news."

The more they tried to hurt President Trump and push lies like Russia collusion, the more he stood strong. Americans had never seen a President with such character and strength in their lifetimes. President Trump withstood their advances and stood strong. He pushed back and pointed out Big Media's lies, and Americans loved him for his honesty and strength.

Many times, people shared with me that they had never seen a person take on so many lies head on. We wondered how he did it and were amazed. He was really withstanding an evil cyclone of lies and not giving in.

The attacks from the media were relentless. They were for the most part lies, and Americans didn't buy it. The more the media pushed against President

222 (Hoft J. , JEROME CORSI: Obama Went After General Flynn Because He Was a Risk of Indicting Him and Hillary for High Crimes and Misdemeanors (PART 2), 2023)

Trump, the more the media's reputation was destroyed. Americans weren't buying the liberal lies.

In *The Steal - Volume I: Setting the Stage,* the term Big Media was used to define what some call the Mainstream Media. Big media refers to the many outlets that are ran by large media corporations throughout the US and the world. Only a few individuals control a large part of the information that reaches the masses, and they own the Big Media corporations.

Poll after poll and study after study conducted before the 2020 Election pointed out the bias in the media and the anti-Trump rage. It was easy to see.

As noted in *The Steal - Volume I: Setting the Stage:*

> Big Media's stories during the Trump years were constantly dishonest, but Big Media's biggest lies were the stories that they did not share.
>
> The media rarely mentioned the beautiful first lady, Melania Trump, who was easily the most graceful and gorgeous first lady in history. Big Media hid from the American people President Trump's many successes that helped the entire country. Regarding these many monumental accomplishments, there was no praise from the media, only crickets.
>
> Thankfully, there were new media like The *Gateway Pundit* and others who filled the void and provided honest coverage of President Trump's many accomplishments as well as Big Media's many lies. This battle for the hearts of good Americans went on every day.

Before the 2020 Election, other than *FOX News*, there were no news channels that came close to reporting fairly on President Trump. Then came November 3, 2020, Election night:

> Most of the Trump crowd were keeping up at *FOX News*. But that network pulled out their biggest Trump haters to report on the results that night. Chris Wallace, who'd already shown his utter disdain for President Trump during the debates, led the group of reporters on the *FOX* channel. Trump supporters like Sean Hannity and others were placed in minor roles. The same occurred at the *FOX Business* channel.

> Neil Cavuto, a Trump hater, led the reporting, while Trump supporters like Maria Bartiromo and Lou Dobbs were relegated to the back of the bus. The final results were never reported that evening. After listening to blowhards Wallace and Cavuto, Americans finally went to bed while several states where President Trump was way ahead were left uncalled.

It wasn't until February of 2023 that we learned that *FOX* was intentionally blocking stories about the 2020 Election steal. Dominion sued *FOX News* after the election in a defamation case and then released information from their depositions in the public realm in 2023. Dominion was attempting to claim that *FOX News* was publishing information on the election steal and released text messages from some of the hosts to make their point.[223]

To the average Trump supporter who watched *FOX News* after the 2020 Election, *FOX* was ignoring the thousands of examples of the corruption and election fraud in the 2020 Election. Information from Dominion's depositions of *FOX News* proved this was the case. Records show that former Republican Speaker of the US House of Representatives, Paul Ryan, was working with the owners and executive team of *FOX* to stop reporting on the election and President Trump. Ryan reportedly gave the top individuals at *FOX* "plenty of suggestions with respect to programming as well as suggestions regarding content and show hosts."[224]

Ryan, who hated President Trump, was doing all he could to destroy him. Dominion shared:[225]

> Specifically, he told the Murdochs that *FOX* should "be pivoting at this key inflection point during November 2020 through January 2021,"

223 (Hoft J. , Court Documents Detail How Paul Ryan Pushed FOX News Owners to "Move on from Trump" Despite Polls Showing Channel Was Losing Its Core Viewers, 2023)

224 Ibid

225 Ibid

consistently advising them "to move on from Donald Trump and stop spouting election lies."

Ryan's actions based on his deep hate for President Trump severely damaged *FOX's* relationship with its base—the massive number of Trump voters—and provided Dominion some ammunition to use against the company in its lawsuit. The only news site that would report honestly on President Trump some of the time after the 2020 Election stopped reporting on the President at all. We knew it was bad in 2021 and could see what was going on; by 2023, we had support for what we saw.

Big Tech

In *The Steal - Volume I: Setting the Stage*, Big Tech was also discussed. This gang of social media giants was instrumental in promoting liberal lies and censoring conservative thought. Free speech was abandoned on these platforms, as they used sections of the law to suggest what they were doing was legal. Morality meant nothing.

In *The Steal - Volume I: Setting the Stage*, it was noted that the leaders of Facebook, Twitter, and Google all claimed a month before the 2020 Election that America would not have an election winner on Election night. How could they all have known this unless they were privy to a plot in place to prevent President Trump from winning the election?

There was evidence that Big Tech had sided with Biden and the Democrats and the Deep State. They all worked together. After the election steal the purge began. Conservatives [*like myself*] who reported on the crimes and seediness on Hunter Biden's laptop before the election and who reported on the election steal after the election were suspended or permanently banned from social media.

Big Tech had begun censoring and shadow banning (when Big Tech partially blocks an individual's shares with his followers; the user doesn't know it, but his followers are not receiving his posts and shares) conservatives even before the 2016 election, but this went into full force in 2017.

By the time the 2020 Election came around, all big conservative targets were censored, shadow banned, or suspended for good. President Trump was clearly shadow banned by this time. He was allowed to keep his accounts and was known as the greatest tweeter in history, but his tweets weren't shared. You had to go to his account to see his tweets. After January 6, Big Tech took down President Trump, their biggest target and their biggest casualty.

We thought that Big Tech companies had operated independently or in collusion with other social media giants in their censoring activities. But this was only a very small piece of the picture. **Deep State actors were involved in the censoring of conservatives alongside Big Tech.** This was big-time collusion.

For years, Big Tech was able to censor and ban certain social media users or groups based on the law known as Section 230.[226]

> The law allows for companies to engage in "good Samaritan" moderation of "objectionable" material without being treated like a publisher or speaker under the law.
>
> That's what allows platforms like Twitter, Facebook, and Google's YouTube to take down terrorist content or harassing messages while still enjoying other legal protections. It's also been essential for these companies to achieve massive scale; if they were liable for everything users posted, they'd either have to vet every piece of content before it went live, which would dramatically increase expenses and create delays, or give up all moderation, which would make for a worse user experience.

What happened over time, however, was that the Big Tech companies took advantage of Section 230 and began targeting conservatives only. As conservatives were shadow banned, suspended, and censored, those on the left were left alone.

---

226 (Feiner, 2020)

It was discovered in the summer of 2020 that President Trump had been censored multiple times on Twitter. Jack Dorsey, Twitter's CEO, was in front of the US Senate, and he lied about it, but there was evidence that President Trump had been censored 65 times. At this point, individuals on Twitter began asking Jack why Iran's Ayatollah, who was calling for violence against the USA, was allowed to maintain an account on Twitter uninhibited, but the President of the United States was censored.[227]

(Note that as of the date of this writing, the tweets that provide support for the Ayatollah being left alone on Twitter and President Trump being censored 65 times have been censored and taken down from Twitter.)

Big Tech began targeting Americans who happened to be conservative, God-loving, and family-loving citizens who were funny, smart, and popular. Americans were losing their first amendment rights to free speech, while Big Tech claimed they were protecting the country. Section 230 was used against Americans, and terrorists were left alone. The "terrorists" Big Tech was targeting were American conservatives.

When Americans tried to sue Big Tech for taking away their first amendment rights, Big Tech would throw down their trump card and claim Section 230. Conservatives knew they were being targeted, but they didn't have the proof to support what appeared clear. Then came Dr. Shiva Ayyadurai.[228]

> Dr. Shiva discovered that Twitter built a special portal offered to certain governmental entities so that government officials could flag and delete content they disliked for any reason, as part of what they call their "Twitter Partner Status."

---

227 (Hoft J. , Jack Dorsey of Twitter Defends Censoring President Trump but not Iran's America Hating Ayatollah, 2020)

228 (Hoft J. , Long Before Elon Musk's Disclosure – Dr. Shiva Ayyadurai Uncovered Twitter's "Partner Support Portal" Used by Democrats, Govt. Officials, and Twitter Associates to Censor Conservatives, 2022)

> Dr. Shiva Ayyadurai, the man who invented email, ran for US Senate in Massachusetts as a Republican and made allegations of voter fraud on Twitter. These tweets were then deleted by the far-left tech giant. Later, it was discovered that they were deleted at the direction of government employees of the Massachusetts Secretary of State's office.
>
> Discovering this, Dr. Ayyadurai filed a federal lawsuit by himself, alleging that his federal civil rights were violated when the government silenced his political speech in order to affect an election.

What Dr. Shiva had uncovered was more than the fact that his tweets were removed from Twitter and that he was being censored unfairly. He uncovered that the US government was working with Twitter to censor his free speech.

Dr. Shiva revealed how election officials and government actors work together to coordinate with social media platforms to silence speech in America. **Certain government agencies forged relationships with billionaires through various funds and other non-governmental organizations to fund, design, and deploy this centralized infrastructure for censorship of speech.**[229]

The Missouri and Louisiana Lawsuit

The information uncovered by Dr. Shiva eventually reached the desks of two state Attorney Generals. Missouri's Attorney General Eric Schmitt and Louisiana's Attorney General Jeff Landry formed an alliance and together in early May of 2022 filed a lawsuit (*Missouri v. Biden*) against the Biden Administration, including Biden himself, Anthony Fauci, the Department of Homeland Security, and nearly a dozen federal agencies and Secretaries.[230]

FOX News reported at the time:[231]

---

229 Ibid

230 (Laila, Republican Attorneys General Sue Joe Biden For Colluding with Big Tech to Censor Information on Hunter's 'Laptop From Hell' and Covid, 2022)

231 (Laco, 2022)

> Missouri Attorney General Eric Schmitt and Louisiana Attorney General Jeff Landry filed the lawsuit Thursday in US District Court for the Western District of Louisiana. The suit accuses top ranking government officials of working with the giant social media companies Meta, Twitter, and YouTube "under the guise of combating misinformation" in order to achieve greater censorship.
>
> The lawsuit names Nina Jankowicz, the head of the Department of Homeland Security's (DHS) new "Disinformation Governance Board," which has received severe backlash from both Democratic and Republican lawmakers for limiting free speech. Lawmakers have expressed concern specifically with the appointment of Jankowicz, who promoted the widely-discredited Christopher Steele dossier and repeated the narrative that Hunter Biden's laptop was a product of a Russian disinformation campaign.
>
> DHS Secretary Alejandro Mayorkas, the Centers for Disease Control and Prevention (CDC), the National Institute of Allergy and Infectious Diseases (NIAID), Department of Health and Human Services (HHS) Secretary Xavier Becerra, Surgeon General Vivek Murthy, and Director of the Cybersecurity and Infrastructure Security Agency Jen Easterly are also named as defendants in the filing.
>
> The lawsuit alleges that the federal government violated constitutional rights to suppress free speech in "one of its greatest assaults by federal government officials in the Nation's history."

The Attorneys General shared numerous instances of the government working with Big Tech and stating that they were working with Big Tech to censor conservative free speech. The Democrats, the government, and Big Tech had no concerns in doing so.[232]

In July of 2022, the Attorneys General received good news when they persuaded the federal judge to grant them limited discovery (investigatory powers) before the court. This allowed the Attorneys General to compel the

232 Op cit, Laila – Republican Attorneys General Sue Joe Biden...

government, Facebook, Twitter, and a few other social media platforms to turn over documents and communications exchanged between them and the government in which censorship was discussed.[233]

After that ruling, the Attorneys General began requesting information and deposing individuals within the government and Big Tech. Numerous government officials including Dr. Tony Fauci were deposed and testified in the case.[234]

Before the depositions were taken and before the documents requested in the lawsuit were received, Big Tech was starting to change their story behind the censoring of American conservatives, the most patriotic and hard-working people in the county. Mark Zuckerberg from Facebook was on with top podcaster Joe Rogan. In his interview, in late August 2022, Zuckerberg casually admitted that Facebook algorithmically censored the Hunter Biden Laptop Story for seven days following a request from the FBI to censor election "misinformation." This was a turning point in the battle for the preservation of the First Amendment and Free Speech in America.[235]

Then the depositions began. Dr. Fauci was deposed and spent a day with the attorneys representing the two states. The questions he was asked were mostly related to his actions in the COVID-19 crisis.[236]

Another individual deposed by the Attorneys General was a little-known State Department employee by the name of Daniel Kimmage, the Acting Coordinator for the Global Engagement Center at the Department of State. During his deposition, Kimmage revealed something shocking and potentially corrupt or even criminal.[237]

---

233 (Hoft J. , NYT Reports On Missouri-Louisiana Lawsuit featuring Gateway Pundit and Esteemed US Doctors Against Government Officials and Agencies Who Censored Our Speech As Lawsuit Comes to a Head, 2023)

234 Ibid

235 (Hoft J. , MAJOR UPDATE: Missouri AG Schmitt's Lawsuit FORCES Zuckerberg to ADMIT the FBI TOLD FACEBOOK TO CENSOR THE BIDEN LAPTOP During the 2020 Election, 2022)

236 (Hoft J. , BREAKING EXCLUSIVE: Daniel Kimmage Deposition By MO and LA AGs Reveals State Department Was Funding Online Fact-Checkers to Censor Speech, 2022)

237 Ibid

In his testimony Kimmage uncovered that **the State Department was funding online fact-checkers**. Kimmage didn't state whether it was foreign or domestic fact-checkers that the State Department was funding, but he did mention the Poynter Group. This is the entity that operates Politifact, one of Big Tech's biggest fact-checkers for misinformation. This entity that focused on the reporting in conservative media was being paid for by the US State Department.[238]

The Twitter Files

In December of 2022, a short time after Elon Musk had taken over Twitter, he began releasing information showing that Twitter was working with the government to censor Americans based on their conservative political beliefs. The first Twitter files drop was on Friday night, December 2, 2022. The series of tweets began with the following:[239]

> The "Twitter Files" tell an incredible story from inside one of the world's largest and most influential social media platforms. It is a Frankensteinian tale of a human-built mechanism grown out the control of its designer.
>
> Twitter in its conception was a brilliant tool for enabling instant mass communication, making a true real-time global conversation possible for the first time.
>
> In an early conception, Twitter more than lived up to its mission statement, giving people "the power to create and share ideas and information instantly, without barriers."
>
> As time progressed, however, the company was slowly forced to add those barriers. Some of the first tools for controlling speech were designed to combat the likes of spam and financial fraudsters . . .

238 Ibid

239 (Laila, BREAKING: HERE IT IS: Elon Musk Reveals Why Twitter Suppressed Hunter Biden 'Laptop From Hell' Story, 2022)

> Both parties had access to these tools. For instance, in 2020, requests from both the Trump White House and the Biden campaign were received and honored. However:
>
> This system wasn't balanced. It was based on contacts. Because Twitter was and is overwhelmingly staffed by people of one political orientation, there were more channels, more ways to complain, open to the left (well, Democrats) than the right.

The author of the first Twitter file was Matt Taibbi, who had a history of running in far-left liberal circles, but even he could see that Twitter was banishing conservatives. At the end of his series of tweets uncovering the liberal bias at Twitter and their attempts to censor any content related to Hunter Biden's laptop when it first came out, Taibbi shared a tweet where Democrat politicians were pushing for more "moderation" because the Bill of Rights is "not absolute." This was damning, and it was only the beginning.[240]

In the second set of "Twitter files," Bari Weiss released evidence that "teams of Twitter employees build blacklists, prevent disfavored tweets from trending, and actively limit the visibility of entire accounts or even trending topics—all in secret, without informing users." She then provided evidence that conservatives were the targets as well as those who spoke out about COVID response mandates.[241]

From the third set of 'Twitter files," we learned that Twitter created a special channel for executives on October 8, 2020, a month before the 2020 Election. In one tweet, Matt Taibbi wrote: [242]

> During this time, executives were also clearly liaising with federal enforcement and intelligence agencies about moderation of election-related content. While we're still at the start of reviewing the

---

240 Ibid

241 (Hoft J. , TWITTER FILES, PT. 2: Documents Reveal Secret Blacklists and Censorship of Conservative Users – Something former Owner Jack Dorsey Said Was Not Happening, 2022)

242 (Laila, BREAKING: Twitter Files Part 3 Released: How Trump Was Removed From Twitter, 2022)

> #TwitterFiles, we're finding out more about these interactions every day.

In another tweet, Taibbi wrote:[243]

> Examining the entire election enforcement Slack, we didn't see one reference to moderation requests from the Trump campaign, the Trump White House, or Republicans generally. We looked. They may exist; we were told they do. However, they were absent here.

In the same series of tweets, there was ample evidence that at the same time Twitter executives were censoring and shadow banning conservatives they showed privilege to far-left causes, Pro-Biden tweets were routinely approved by Twitter leadership.[244]

In response to the third set of "Twitter files," Missouri's Attorney General Eric Schmitt sent a letter to Twitter, accusing the leadership team there before Musk's takeover of not being truthful in their replies to the Attorney General in his suit against Big Tech and the government. Schmitt demanded that Twitter turn over all of the evidence showing the FBI and DHS's collusion with Twitter. Schmitt noted that these efforts silenced the speech of tens of thousands of Americans, shut down the Hunter Biden Laptop Story, and removed President Trump from Twitter.[245]

Shortly after the Missouri Attorney General's office sent out that letter, Musk and Taibbi started to unveil a fresh batch of evidence that demonstrated that workers at Twitter, including Yoel Roth, were gleefully meeting with the FBI and DHS regularly to receive their marching orders (so long as it agreed with their hard left communist worldview).[246]

---

243 Ibid

244 Ibid

245 (Hoft J. , CAUGHT IN LIES: Latest Twitter Files Release Reveals Feds and Twitter Both Caught Lying, Hiding Evidence in Major Lawsuit; Missouri Attorney General Eric Schmitt Calls Them Onto the Carpet, 2022)

246 Ibid

On Christmas Eve, 2022, another batch of Twitter files were released. In one tweet from Matt Taibbi, he shared that "Twitter had so much contact with so many agencies that executives lost track. Is today the DOD, and tomorrow the FBI? Is it the weekly call, or the monthly meeting? It was dizzying."[247]

One thing Twitter and the FBI didn't lose track of was the amount of money the FBI was paying Twitter. James Baker was Jim Comey's top attorney at the FBI when the fake Trump-Russia collusion lie was perpetrated on the President and the American people in a seditious attempt to have President Trump removed from office. Baker left the FBI and landed at Twitter as its Deputy General Counsel. In 2019, Baker received a message from an associate at Twitter stating that **Twitter had received over $3.4 million from the FBI** for their work with the FBI in censoring conservatives.[248]

Numerous other tweets were released showing Twitter's relationship with government agencies and politicians. California's corrupt and ever-lying Adam Schiff even contacted Twitter to censor a reporter. The list of abuse and criminal activity involving Big Tech and the government goes on and on.[249]

By March of 2023, the journalists given access to the records at Twitter came to this conclusion: "We came to think of this grouping—state agencies like DHS, FBI, or the Global Engagement Center (GEC), along with "NGOs that aren't academic" and an unexpectedly aggressive partner, commercial news media—as the **Censorship-Industrial Complex**."[250]

US House Representative Matt Gaetz discussed this "censorship-industrial complex" with Twitter files journalists Matt Taibbi and Michael Shellenberger, calling it a growth industry. Gaetz poetically shared:[251]

---

247 (Laila, JUST IN: Another Twitter Files Drop: Twitter and "Other Government Agencies", 2022)

248 (Hoft J. , FBI Paid Twitter $3.4 Million in US Tax Dollars for Administration Costs Related to the Staff's Time Spent Working with the FBI, 2022)

249 (Laila, JUST IN: Another 'Twitter Files' Drop: More Adam Schiff Ban Requests – Twitter "Deamplified" Alleged Conservative Accounts They Say Were Linked to Q-Anon, 2023)

250 (Laila, Matt Taibbi Drops Another Twitter Files Ahead of Testimony to Congress: The Censorship-Industrial Complex, 2023)

251 (Hoft J. , "This Censorship Industrial Complex is a Growth Industry to the Government" – Rep. Matt Gaetz on Government Funded Censorship of Conservatives, 2023)

> The nexus to authoritarianism is the desire to control the nature of truth itself. That is the true goal of the Censorship-Industrial Complex.

Gaetz, Taibbi, and Shellenberger went on to discuss how the Department of Defense was paying "fact checker" Newsguard "not only to seek content moderation but apply subjective risk or reliability scores to media outlets," which would result in a reduction of revenue for conservative publishers.[252]

Gaetz, Taibbi, and Shellenberger also discussed the Secretary of State's Global Engagement Center (GEC). The **GEC helped fund Newsguard** along with the Department of Defense. The GEC is also instrumental in funding other entities focused on censoring conservative media and the truth.[253]

In another report, it was discovered that the GEC was funding a censorship entity out of the UK that was targeting conservative media in the US. The US taxpayer-funded National Endowment for Democracy and the State Department's **GEC funded over $600,000 to the UK's Global Disinformation Index (GDI)**. Other high-profile funders of the GDI are George Soros's Open Society, the European Union, and the United Kingdom. The GDI openly bragged about attacking conservative media advertisers and preventing them from supporting these entities.[254]

The Election Integrity Project

The Election Integrity Project (EIP) is another entity that has emerged before, during, and after the 2020 election. This entity was so proud of its work during this time period that it came out with a report where it bragged about censoring conservatives.[255]

---

252 Ibid

253 Ibid

254 (Hoft J. , BOMBSHELL REVELATION: State Department's GEC, Soros's Open Society, the EU, and UK Are Funding the "Disinformation Index": A Pseudo-Nonprofit that "Blacklists" Conservative News from Online Advertisers, 2023)

255 (Hoft J. , EXCLUSIVE: Radical Far-Left Group (EIP) Created Partnership with Government and Social Media to Censor and Ban Any 2020 Election Reporting – The

The EIP was a partnership of far-left zealots from government, Big Tech, and leftist organizations who claimed exclusive ownership of the "truth" and attacked any reporting that indicated the 2020 Election was stolen. The EIP was initially funded by the government (the CISA) and a Stanford University related entity to address any expected complaints in the upcoming election. The Atlantic Council and Graphika were two other entities that were involved.[256]

Figure 1.3: Major stakeholder groups that collaborated with the EIP.

The *Gateway Pundit* was one of the most targeted sites according to the EIP report. The main subject matter attacked was related to the 2020 Election. Those involved in the 2020 Election steal could not allow the truth to get out. Numerous entities worked together to make sure it never did.[257]

Gateway Pundit Was Top Target, 2022)

256 Ibid

257 Ibid

9

The Non-Election System Secret

In February 2023, the House Oversight Committee held a meeting with Twitter executives concerning government and Big Tech collusion and suppression of free speech regarding the Hunter Biden laptop. Florida Representative Anna Paulina Luna was a member on the committee, and she destroyed the Twitter executives during her questioning.[258]

Luna was exceptional, as she exposed the hidden network operating in the dark that is destroying free speech in America. The network includes the DHS, CISA, DFITF, EIP, CIS, and others. Luna brought proof that Yoel Roth from Twitter was using the private software cloud JIRA to communicate with the FBI and government officials to silence conservative speech.[259]

In her chart, Representative Luna shared that Big Tech communicates with various entities using Jira. Two entities that Big Tech communicates with listed in this chart were the Cybersecurity Infrastructure and Security Agency (CISA), which is housed under the Department of Homeland Security (DHS),

---

258 (Hoft J. , A STAR IS BORN! Rep. Anna Paulina Luna TORCHES Yoel Roth – Exposes Democrat-Big Tech-Government Collusion and Former TWITTER EXECS ARE LEFT SPEECHLESS!, 2023)

259 Ibid

and the Countering Foreign Influence Task Force (CFITF), which is under CISA.[260]

The Election Integrity Project (EIP) was created before the 2020 Election, as was noted above. The entity worked with the Stanford Internet Observatory, Graphika, and the Atlantic Council. It also worked with the University of Washington's Center for Informed Public.[261]

The Center for Internet Security (CIS) was identified on Rep. Luna's chart. This entity, as we will see, is very much involved in elections as well as the National Association of Secretaries of State (NASS) and the National Association of State Election Directors (NASED). These two state entities were discussed in *The Steal - Volume I: Setting the Stage*. We had no idea how well connected these entities were.

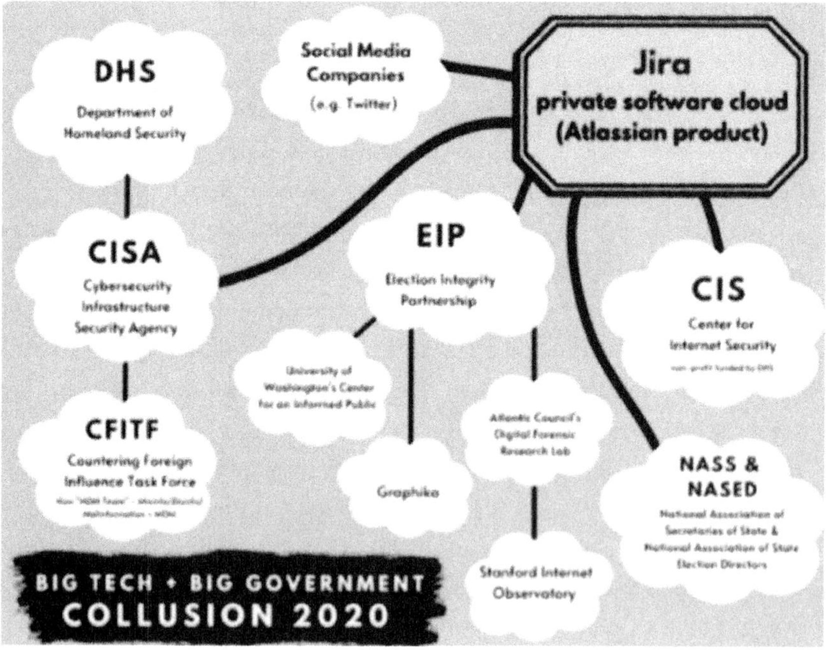

---

260 Ibid

261 Ibid

What was soon uncovered was that these same entities involved in censoring conservatives are also major spokes in the election steal wheel.

NEW MEXICO ELECTIONS

As noted previously, Attorney David Clements and his wife Erin Clements were instrumental in seeing to it that an audit of the 2020 results was performed in New Mexico. There were many players behind the audit, along with many patriots who supported the effort with their time and energy. The audit produced results that questioned patterns in voter rolls. Canvassing work was also performed with results similar to other states, where a material number of votes were suspect. New Mexico is also one of the seven states that sent two sets of electors to Washington DC on January 6 because the 2020 results in the state were suspected of being corrupted.

New Mexico's Secretary of State is Soros-backed Maggie Toulouse-Oliver. In a March 10, 2023, hearing in the New Mexico House Judiciary Committee on the controversial election bill titled SB 180, Representative Greg Nibert asked the Secretary of State directly, "Is the election system connected to the Internet?"[262]

Toulouse-Oliver's representation to the legislature was false. She claimed that the election system was not connected to the Internet. The truth is that the SOS went to great lengths and spent almost $3 million of taxpayer dollars to get almost the entire election system centralized under her control and exposed to the Internet. The clerks and the Secretary of State also worked with Dominion Voting Systems to destroy all original electronic election data, which prevented a review of the state's results.[263]

262 (Hoft J. , Soros-Backed NM SOS Caught Lying to Legislature – NM Election System Completely Exposed to the Internet, 2023)

263 Ibid

A team in New Mexico determined that the post-election canvass reports in all 33 New Mexico Counties were being **illegally prepared**.[264]

> Complete election records were uploaded to an uncertified, centralized software under the control of the SOS called SERVIS, which is then used to create the official election results. Use of any uncertified software for this part of the election process is a violation of federal and state law. And according to state law, the SOS is not to have access to the complete election record from any county until the election has been certified.

The results in New Mexico were pushed through the system named SERVIS before certifying the results. The counties in the state downloaded election data from Internet connected SERVIS onto their "secure" election computers, and then Dominion came in and wiped out the original election data on their devices, which prevented a reconciliation of original data entries on Dominion systems with the SERVIS data that was provided to the counties. This was a blatant violation of state and federal law that requires all election records to be kept for 22 months after any election with a federal candidate on the ballot.[265]

It was then discovered that SERVIS was the local name for the TotalVote election system provided by a vendor by the name of BPro. According to the BPro website, TotalVote is a:[266]

> . . . centralized voter registration and election management system that securely captures and manages voter, candidate, and all election information. It is the only software system that encompasses the entire election process into one system.

---

264 Ibid

265 Ibid

266 (BPro.com, 2023)

The Election Assistance Commission (EAC) does not certify TotalVote whatsoever. This means TotalVote does not comply with the Help America Vote Act (HAVA), and it has never been tested by any EAC "accredited" third-party[267] (see *The Steal - Volume II: The Impossible Occurs* for a discussion on EAC "accredited" auditors and the certification process).

NON-VOTING SYSTEMS

The discovery of BPro's TotalVote used in New Mexico led to more questions. Election experts in New Mexico established that the post-election canvass reports in all 33 New Mexico Counties were illegally prepared because complete election records were uploaded to an uncertified, centralized software under the control of the Secretary of State (SOS) called SERVIS, which is then used to create the official election results. This led to questions about BPro and where else its TotalVote was being used.[268]

About the time that BPro's TotalVote was identified as in use in New Mexico, it was identified as in use in Hawaii, where Hawaiian experts believed the system allowed for backdated entries in voter rolls. Also, a contract between BPro and the state of Pennsylvania was identified from 2020 where the contract stated that: "BPro's TotalVote solution was designed as a centralized, statewide top-down system." The contract also noted that TotalVote was fully integrated with ERIC, the voter registration system used by many states across the country.[269]

BPro was purchased by KNOWiNK shortly after the 2020 Election. These combined entities reported their shared software can be found in **36 states across the country**.[270]

---

267 Op cit, Soros Backed NM SOS Caught…

268 (Hoft J. , State-Wide Top-Down System" Used in Multiple States Is Internet Connected, Non-Certified, Connects with Dominion and ERIC, and Allows "Plug-Ins" That Can Change Results – And No One Has Reported on This Until Now, 2023)

269 Ibid

270 Ibid

KNOWiNK promotes several election products on its site. It has a platform for voter registration as well as poll pads, devices that look like Apple iPads with election software loaded onto them that are used to sign in voters during elections. Access to this data would likely tell the user who has voted on election day and where they voted.[271]

Apparently, this information is accumulated because KNOWiNK also has a platform that provides users real-time access to elections. This module apparently provides customers with the **ability to see detailed information on election night** for candidates who are leading in races in the states where the platform is used. In addition, another platform allows for the printing of ballots on-site.[272]

It was then uncovered that there were at least two companies that had election system software and platforms similar to KNOWiNK. Tenex Software Solutions and VR Systems advertise similar election solutions on their websites. Combined, these companies cover much of the US. Surprisingly, these entities and their systems were rarely discussed when the 2020 Election occurred.

What quickly became evident about these systems is that they are not certified by any government entity. These systems are referred to as "non-voting" systems and somehow not considered related to elections, so they are not included in the EAC's scope of election systems. Election systems like Dominion and ES&S were to be certified by accredited voter system testing labs. However, these labs do not test these non-voting systems, nor do they likely have the expertise to do so.

The CIS and Albert Sensors

One big question when reviewing these non-voting systems was how the manufacturers obtained the data they advertise as having available. It's not hard to imagine that these systems would obtain access to the poll pad data. This would provide the "real-time" results these manufacturers provide. Having

271 (KNOWiNK.com, 2023)

272 Ibid

access to the poll pads would tell you who voted (a Republican, Democrat, or Independent), where they voted, and when they voted. With this information, bad actors could fix an election if they had the ability to do so.

But what if the data did not come from the poll pads? Where else could it come from? Maybe it comes from the government?[273]

> The Department of Homeland Security's private partner, Center for Internet Security (CIS), installed "Albert Sensors" all over the United States to monitor real-time data in election jurisdictions down to the county level. The program was present in only a handful of states in 2016 but was massively expanded after Donald Trump's 2016 upset victory over Hillary Clinton.
>
> While Albert Sensors quickly proliferated across the United States' election infrastructure, CIS worked with left-wing NGOs, election officials, and Twitter to set up a powerful censorship operation to squash all discussion of irregularities and fraud observed in the 2020 election.

Perhaps the censorship activities targeting conservative media were only a small part of the overall election steal?

The same CIS that was identified by GOP Rep. Luna in the hearing with Twitter executives as central to the censorship of conservative media is also heavily involved in the non-voting systems prevalent across the US. The CIS piloted a faux-certification program called **RABET-V**—where they hired the owner of an electronic ballot delivery company to lead an effort to conclude that the nation's "non-voting technology" (i.e., electronic pollbooks, election night reporting, etc.) are "safe and secure."[274]

Ironically, after the article about the RABET-V program was posted, an individual on Twitter tweeted on a document showing that the RABET-V

273 (Hoft J. , EXCLUSIVE: Far-Left NGO 'Democracy Fund' Financed Efforts to Certify "Non-Voting Technology" and Use It to Monitor Elections on a Real-Time Basis, 2023)

274 Ibid

initiative at the CIS was funded by the far-left Democracy Fund. This tweet was censored within a couple of hours.[275]

The RABET-V pilot technology partners include Electronic Systems & Software (ES&S), Runbeck, KNOWiNK (owner of BPro), and VR Systems. The state of South Carolina donated its voter registration system to the project. **Almost all of these companies have been highlighted in election integrity investigations and by independent auditors in their investigations into the 2020 Election.**[276]

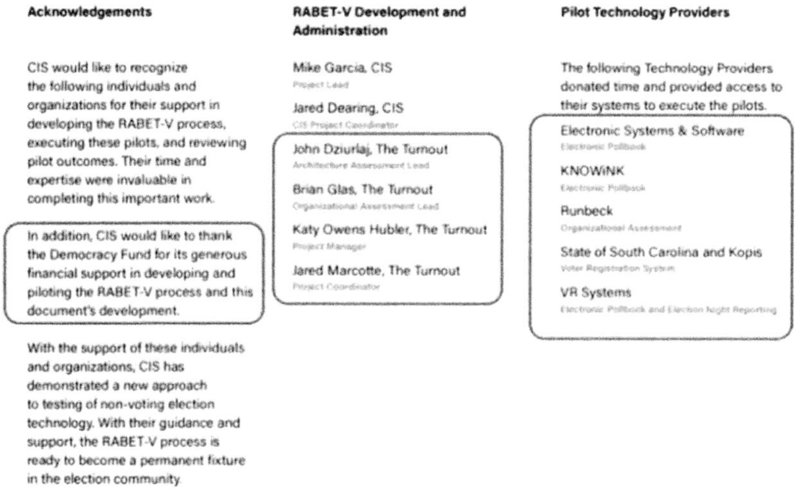

Acknowledgements

CIS would like to recognize the following individuals and organizations for their support in developing the RABET-V process, executing these pilots, and reviewing pilot outcomes. Their time and expertise were invaluable in completing this important work.

In addition, CIS would like to thank the Democracy Fund for its generous financial support in developing and piloting the RABET-V process and this document's development.

With the support of these individuals and organizations, CIS has demonstrated a new approach to testing of non-voting election technology. With their guidance and support, the RABET-V process is ready to become a permanent fixture in the election community.

RABET-V Development and Administration

Mike Garcia, CIS
Project Lead

Jared Dearing, CIS
CIS Project Coordinator

John Dziurlaj, The Turnout
Architecture Assessment Lead

Brian Glas, The Turnout
Organizational Assessment Lead

Katy Owens Hubler, The Turnout
Project Manager

Jared Marcotte, The Turnout
Project Coordinator

Pilot Technology Providers

The following Technology Providers donated time and provided access to their systems to execute the pilots.

Electronic Systems & Software
Electronic Pollbook

KNOWiNK
Electronic Pollbook

Runbeck
Organizational Assessment

State of South Carolina and Kopis
Voter Registration System

VR Systems
Electronic Pollbook and Election Night Reporting

Excerpt from CIS's "RABET-V Final Pilot Summary and Next Steps"

The team that developed and administered the RABET-V program had two representatives from CIS, and the rest were from a shadowy company called "The Turnout," for which very little information is available. The Democracy Fund is run by billionaire Pierre Omidyar, one of the largest contributors to

275 Ibid

276 Ibid

far-left anti-American causes and a major contributor to the efforts to crack down on conservative speech in America.[277]

To this day, the services provided by the non-election system companies are still in place. The Albert Sensors are still in place as well. The fact that the CIS is not a government entity prevents the public from obtaining information that government entities would be mandated to provide. This is the perfect storm waiting to strike.

Corrupt Senator Warner's Election Bill

In March of 2023, Virginia's corrupt Democrat Senator Mark Warner introduced his RESTRICT Act. This Act was supported by Democrat Senators and Republican Senators like Thune, Collins, and Romney. The Act claims to restrict activities between US and foreign entities, but it goes much further than that.[278]

Warner's RESTRICT Act increases the federal government's ability to spy on Americans' online activity and punish them for sharing information that opposes the official narrative. But what hasn't been noticed is that the RESTRICT Act will provide the federal government with enormous control over American elections. The Act will lay out enforcement of any mitigation effort in response to individuals or entities "interfering in or altering the result or reported result of a federal election, as determined in coordination with the Attorney General, the Director of National Intelligence, the Secretary of Treasury, and the Federal Election Commission."[279]

Once the ability to steal elections is in place, every good communist knows you need to keep it that way.

---

277 Ibid

278 (Warner, 2023)

279 (Hoft J. , EXCLUSIVE: Corrupt Senator Mark Warner's "Restrict Act" Is the Patriot Act for Elections that Gives the Government Enormous Power – Forcing Counties to Enable "Albert Sensors" or Mandate Other Sinister Election Activities, 2023)

10

What's Next

If someone were to ask you, "How do you know the Presidential Election of 2020 was stolen," there is one simple answer that you can provide in one sentence:

The 2020 Election should have never been certified, and as a result, it was stolen from President Trump and America.

There is ample evidence in *The Steal - Volume II: The Impossible Occurs* to support the above statement. But what is more important and scarier is what is coming next.

The 2020 Election for President of the United States will go down as one of the most tragic and nefarious events in world history. Maybe 1000 years from now, a great writer will put together the tragedy of the stolen 2020 Election like Shakespeare did with the death of Julius Caesar.

Setting the Stage

There were many issues with the 2020 Election. In *The Steal - Volume I: Setting the Stage*, a list of entities and their actions before the 2020 Election were identified and recorded. Planning for the 2020 Election steal went on for months, if not years. The 2020 Election steal was no mistake.

For more than four years, candidate and then-President Trump was under attack by the Deep State. These corrupt actors in the government did all they could to derail his campaign and then remove him from office when he won. The Trump Administration faced a coup, and only President Trump's strength and knowledge that he did nothing wrong prevented him from being removed from office.

When the initial stages of the coup were unsuccessful in removing President Trump from office, a new plan was put in place. This effort was reminiscent of the "color revolutions" the CIA had performed in countries around the world to implement a regime change. Before the 2020 Election, Americans were warned, and after the election, the Deep State patted themselves on the back for their removal of President Trump from office.

Big Tech forewarned US voters that the results of the election would not be available on election night. This was something that hadn't happened in the modern era. Big Tech also attacked President Trump and conservative media and eventually shadow banned and censored even President Trump.

Big Media was also a big part of the coup. The legacy media monsters pushed the narrative "Orange Man Bad" in every broadcast possible for four years. After the 2020 Election, Big Media labeled Joe Biden "President-elect" and President Trump "former President Trump." This mantra was consistent and constant.

Foreign powers like China didn't want another four years of President Trump. In early 2020, COVID was released in China. Much of this has been ignored by Big Media and US politicians, but it was real, and it did impact the US economy and the 2020 Election. If China did do this intentionally, it was because President Trump was destroying the Chinese economy. It's clear now, after all the revelations of the Bidens' deals with China, that China wanted Joe Biden in the Presidency and not President Trump.

COVID was also used as an excuse to push for absentee mail-in ballots across the country in the 2020 Election. Americans couldn't be around each other; the postal service would have to handle millions of ballots in the election. This alone opened the door for a huge opportunity for election fraud and much of it wasn't constitutional since it hadn't been approved by the legislatures.

Multiple non-profits were formed before and leading up to the 2020 Election. Millions was provided to these entities and from these entities to some of the most crooked actors the country has ever seen, all to ensure Joe Biden was "elected" President.

Biden was a horrible candidate. He embodied more things that Americans hated than what they wanted. Biden was in government his entire life. He and his family were connected to corruption around the world. In addition, he was old and senile. Yet, he was the best the Democrats had. Biden stayed in his basement most of his campaign and rarely came out. When Biden did do a "rally," it was in a small setting with circles on the floor for 12 or more "guests." While Biden entertained a few bored people in circles, President Trump entertained more than a million at huge venues across the country.

THE IMPOSSIBLE OCCURS

In *The Steal - Volume II: The Impossible Occurs*, an inventory of issues, actions, inactions, crimes, and fraudulent activities were presented that all led to Biden's win.

The election should have ended when poll watchers were physically kicked out of precincts and locations where ballots were being counted. The fact that law enforcement allowed this to happen indicated in some instances that they were in on it. This was a national disgrace. The elections where this happened should have ended right then and there, but instead, these actions were ignored, and the counts generated behind closed doors were certified.

The numbers behind the election never made sense. How could President Trump win all but one of the bellwether counties in the election, for example, and yet Biden win the election? Numerous anomalies at the nation, state, and county level were presented, and based on the numbers, President Trump should have won in a landslide. Something was very wrong.

When experts began looking at the resulting data from the election, they identified that the data had patterns in it that indicated some sort of manipulation going on. Experts looked at the data and could see that where these patterns were present something was awry. What was going on?

Next, it was determined that over a million ballots entered the election in swing states, and we have no idea where they came from. These ballots were counted, yet no "chain of custody" records were connected to them. They should have been discarded.

Similarly, for millions of ballots in swing states, signature verifications were not performed and were virtually turned off across the country. In an election with the most mail-in ballots in history, the validity of the ballots was basically not determined, and yet, the ballots were counted.

The systems used in the election were to be certified per the laws in many states, but this certification was performed by entities not properly accredited. Compliance with applicable election laws in numerous states was not in place.

Election systems put in place in the election had numerous issues. Experts had been warning us for years that the election machines had serious and material flaws, but no one listened. The CISA issued a report as a result of an audit performed after the 2020 Election, telling us that the election systems have many gaps in security that would allow bad actors to manipulate data in an election. The election systems appeared to have been built this way by design.

Multiple entities, governments, and individuals colluded to ensure Joe Biden would win in the 2020 Election. Big Media, Big Tech, state and local governments, companies, and non-profits all worked in unison to make certain this was the case.

Looking back, America's strongest (the military), America's weakest (the elderly in retirement homes), and everyone in between was susceptible to fraudulent activities in the 2020 Election steal.

The Cover-up

The steal had to be covered up immediately. This cover-up of the 2020 Election steal began as soon as counting started in polling locations across the country, but this was all planned well in advance.

The night of the election, law enforcement was missing. A white van and car showed up at the counting center in Detroit and unloaded what appeared to be thousands of ballots underneath the counting area. This happened in the middle of the night, hours after the last check of drop boxes in Detroit. Other incidents were reported across the country. As counting started, GOP poll watchers were prevented physically from performing their duties. At this point, the local sheriffs should have stepped in, but they didn't. The DOJ and FBI should have stepped in, but they didn't. Individuals were getting away with counting ballots behind closed doors, and law enforcement did nothing.

When it became apparent that law enforcement and election directors were going to include tainted ballots in official results, President Trump turned to his smart and loyal friend, Rudy Giuliani, to expose these votes and persuade legislatures in swing states to not certify them. Rudy and his team provided numerous witnesses and over 1,000 affidavits of election wrongdoing to the legislatures in Pennsylvania, Arizona, Michigan, and Georgia. The presentations were compelling, but the GOP-led legislatures were not swayed.

The courts were next. Multiple cases landed in federal courts but many of these landed in front of Obama judges. Three out of four of attorney Sidney Powell's cases providing ample evidence of election fraud in Arizona, Wisconsin, and Michigan hit brick walls when the Obama judges ignored the evidence and used their courts to lambast Powell. The largest case in the land, out of Texas against multiple swing states was thrown out by the Supreme Court. Nearly the entire county was involved in that case, but the Supreme Court refused to hear it.

President Trump and Americans who supported him refused to give up. A rally was scheduled at the Capitol on January 6, 2021. An estimated million people showed up to support President Trump, something Biden would never see. The hope was that Vice President Mike Pence would request that the results in multiple swing states be sent back to the legislatures in those states to review and vote on the delegates that best represented the results in those states. But this never happened.

A riot broke out at the Capitol while President Trump completed his speech a couple miles away at the Ellipse. Four Trump supporters were killed that day. Numerous federal agents and related parties were later identified in the crowd at the Capitol instigating the riots. Congress shut down during the riots, and then later that night, the results of the 2020 Election were approved, and Biden was awarded the election win.

The Democrats and many GOP politicians immediately used the riots to target and imprison Trump supporters and to claim that President Trump attempted to overthrow the government. Based on the information we have today, this was not only a lie but a total projection. The sedition occurred during President Trump's entire administration by the Deep State in the many efforts to remove him from office. The stolen 2020 Election was the ultimate act of sedition, not Jan 6.

Americans refused to accept the fraudulent results from the 2020 Election. They called for audits of the election results. Finally, legislatures agreed to perform audits in various states. The work done in New Hampshire proved to be a waste of time and resources. However, the results in Michigan provided evidence that the voting systems had issues. The Arizona audit in Maricopa County provided ample evidence that the 2020 Election results in the state were not accurate. In New Mexico, the results showed numerous anomalies in the election process. These audits in Michigan, Arizona, and New Mexico provided ample evidence that the elections in those locations were not accurate or reliable, but nothing was done. No legislature had the courage to do anything with these results.

A year after these audits were performed Hunter Biden's laptop was back in the news. It turned out that the 50+ intelligence leaders who claimed before the 2020 Election that the laptop was Russian disinformation had lied. Russia had nothing to do with the laptop. By covering up this information, the US government—not Russia—had interfered in the 2020 Election.

America also learned of the total corruption across the entire government two years after the 2020 Election. Big Tech and Big Media worked in tandem after the 2020 Election to create the false narrative that Joe Biden won the election fair and square. It was uncovered that the federal government was involved in operations to censor conservative media at this same time. This was soon referred to as the censorship-industrial complex, but this was only part of it. The censorship was put in place to cover-up the election steal. The steal was the crime, and censorship was only a part of it.

Two years after the 2020 Election more and more information was still coming out. Election systems unknown about two years prior was discovered to be in use across the country. These new systems had modules for voter roll manipulation, election night status updates, ballot printing on demand and more. These unaudited systems are being put in use and most Americans have no idea what they are used for or if it's even legal.

THE TRUTH

The 2020 Election was not the safest and most secure election ever. The three volumes of *The Steal* show without a doubt that the 2020 Election was stolen. The election was stolen, because it never should have been certified.

We also know that based on the mountains of evidence and a review of events, the 2020 Election steal was well thought through and planned out. This mess of an election did not happen haphazardly. It was designed for the steal.

This was a crime, and the criminals behind this crime knew what they were doing. Joe Biden did not earn more valid votes than President Trump in 2020. He barely made it out of his basement. Americans and the world knew it then and know it now.

President Trump beat Joe Biden by a landslide when counting only valid votes. The problem was that invalid votes were included in the election results.

The 2020 Election should have never been certified, and as a result, it was stolen from President Trump and America.

WHAT'S NEXT?

The 2024 Election steal is already in the works. Those who stole the 2020 Election are working very hard to ensure a 2024 win for whichever candidate they choose.

Like Nazis and communists, the regime that stole the 2020 Election is now after its political enemies. As of early May 2023, these same characters aren't worried about the 2024 Election. They act like they already have won the 2024 Election.

Much work must be done to prevent an election steal in 2024 like what happened in 2020. The 2020 Election was not legitimate; it was stolen.

The corrupt regime in power wants to indict President Trump for treason, and they plan to do it in a DC court. They are coming after him from many directions. They want him punished and destroyed. We are next.

This great nation is under an attack never seen before. Some Americans don't see it. They soon will. The 2024 Election is our last hope if we even make it to the election. A Trump indictment could realistically destroy this country. This is what the evil regime wants. A world without America is a world without hope.

We must work like the 2024 Election win depends on us and pray like the 2024 Election win depends on God.

BIBLIOGRAPHY

Benveniste, A. (2020, October 18). *The anatomy of the New York Post's dubious Hunter Biden story.* Retrieved from CNN.com: https://www.cnn.com/2020/10/18/media/new-york-post-hunter-biden-reliable/index.html

Bertrand, N. (2020, October 19). *Hunter Biden story is Russian disinfo, dozens of former intel officials say.* Retrieved from Politico.com: https://www.politico.com/news/2020/10/19/hunter-biden-story-russian-disinfo-430276

Bobb, C. (2023). Stealing Your Vote - The Inside Story of the 2020 Election and What It Means for 2024. In C. Bobb, *Stealing Your Vote - The Inside Story of the 2020 Election and What It Means for 2024* (p. 67). New York, New York: Skyhorse Publishing.

BPro.com. (2023, May 8). *BPro.com.* Retrieved from BPro.com: https://bpro.com/

Castronuova, C. (2021, November 22). *MUST-READ EXCLUSIVE! Family of Rosanne Boyland Who was KILLED on January 6th Is DENIED HER FULL AUTOPSY REPORT – Speak Out for First Time and Plead for Government Investigation — PLEASE HELP THE BOYLAND FAMILY HERE!* . Retrieved from TheGatewayPundit.com: https://www.thegatewaypundit.com/2021/11/must-read-exclusive-family-rosanne-boyland-killed-january-6th-denied-full-autopsy-report-speak-first-time-plead-government-investigation-please-help-gri/

Committee, U. H. (2023, April 20). *Chairmen Jordan and Turner Demand Documents and Communications from Blinken.* Retrieved from Judiciary,House.gov: https://judiciary.house.gov/media/press-releases/new-testimony-reveals-secretary-blinken-and-biden-campaign-behind-infamous

Diaz, J. (2021, January 11). *Ex-Capitol Police Chief Says Requests For National Guard Denied 6 Times In Riots.* Retrieved from NPR.org: https://www.npr.org/2021/01/11/955548910/ex-capitol-police-chief-rebuffs-claims-national-guard-was-never-called-during-ri

Durkee, A. (2021, January 6). *Sen. Ted Cruz, House GOP Object To Arizona's Electoral Votes.* Retrieved from Forbes.com: https://www.forbes.com/sites/alisondurkee/2021/01/06/sen-ted-cruz-house-gop-republicans-object-to-arizona-electoral-votes-congress/?sh=4e725c3c1ba6

Feiner, L. (2020, February 19). *Big Tech's favorite law is under fire.* Retrieved from CNBC.com: https://www.cnbc.com/2020/02/19/what-is-section-230-and-why-do-some-people-want-to-change-it.html

Flynn, M. (2021, July 30). *Gen. Flynn Exclusive: 10 INDISPUTABLE FACTS on the 2020 Election That Argue for Audits.* Retrieved from WesternJournal.com: https://www.westernjournal.com/gen-flynn-exclusive-10-indisputable-facts-2020-election-argue-audits/

Fonrouge, E.-J. M. (2020, October 14). *Smoking-gun email reveals how Hunter Biden introduced Ukrainian businessman to VP dad.* Retrieved from NYPost.com: https://nypost.com/2020/10/14/email-reveals-how-hunter-biden-introduced-ukrainian-biz-man-to-dad/

Hoft, J. (2020, November 18). *"Drop and Roll" — How The 2020 Election Was Stolen From President Donald Trump (Video).* Retrieved from TheGatewayPundit.com: https://www.thegatewaypundit.com/2020/11/drop-roll-2020-election-stolen-president-donald-trump-video/

Hoft, J. (2020, November 21). *"Georgia Is the First State I'm Going to Blow Up and Mr. Kemp and the Secretary of State Need to Go With It!" — Sidney Powell Releases the Kraken!* Retrieved from TheGatewayPundit.com: https://

www.thegatewaypundit.com/2020/11/georgia-first-state-going-blow-mr-kemp-secretary-state-need-go-sidney-powell-releases-kraken-video/

Hoft, J. (2020, December 2). *"I Can't Get a Job Any More Because Democrats Like to Ruin Your Life!" – GOP Witness GOES OFF at Michigan Hearing (VIDEO).* Retrieved from TheGatewayPundit.com: https://www.thegatewaypundit.com/2020/12/cant-get-job-democrats-like-ruin-life-gop-witness-goes-off-michigan-hearing-video/

Hoft, J. (2020, December 6). *"The FBI Is Nowhere to be Found!" – Rudy Giuliani Reveals UNDENIABLE VOTER FRAUD in 2020 Election – Now Has 1,000 Signed Witness Affidavits! (VIDEO).* Retrieved from TheGatewayPundit.com: https://www.thegatewaypundit.com/2020/12/fbi-nowhere-found-rudy-giuliani-reveals-undeniable-voter-fraud-2020-election-sunday-morning-futures-video/

Hoft, J. (2020, December 11). *"The US Constitution Is Hanging in the Balance Here" – Rush Limbaugh Lays Out Historic Significance of Texas SCOTUS Lawsuit.* Retrieved from TheGatewayPundit.com: https://www.thegatewaypundit.com/2020/12/us-constitution-hanging-balance-rush-limbaugh-lays-historic-significance-texas-scotus-lawsuit/

Hoft, J. (2020, November 25). *"This is Going to Be Your Crowning Achievement!" – Pennsylvania Crowd APPLAUDS President Trump and Rudy Giuliani — Start Chanting, "Trump! Trump! Trump!..." at Gettysburg Hearing (VIDEO).* Retrieved from TheGatewayPundit.com: https://www.thegatewaypundit.com/2020/11/pennsylvania-crowd-applauds-president-trump-rudy-giuliani-start-chanting-trump-trump-trump-gettysburg-hearing/

Hoft, J. (2020, October 20). *50 Former Intel Officials Including Clapper and Brennan Sign Letter Saying Hunter Biden Emails Story is Russian Disinformation — Despite DNI Ratcliffe's Statement.* Retrieved from TheGatewayPundit.com:

https://www.thegatewaypundit.com/2020/10/50-former-intel-officials-including-clapper-brennan-sign-letter-saying-hunter-biden-emails-story-russian-disinformation-despite-dni-ratcliffes-statement/

Hoft, J. (2020, October 28). *BREAKING EXCLUSIVE: Hunter Biden Held Inappropriate Pictures of Certain Minor — Joe Biden Is Lying*. Retrieved from TheGatewayPundit.com: https://www.thegatewaypundit.com/2020/10/breaking-exclusive-hunter-biden-pictures-half-naked-exposed-certain-minor-joe-biden-lying/

Hoft, J. (2020, October 27). *BREAKING EXCLUSIVE: Hunter Biden's "RUSSIAN BLACKMAIL PHOTOS" Uncovered – Hunter with Russians in Hollywood*. Retrieved from TheGatewayPundit.com: https://www.thegatewaypundit.com/2020/10/breaking-exclusive-hunter-bidens-russian-blackmail-photos-uncovered-hunter-russians-hollywood/

Hoft, J. (2020, October 26). *BREAKING EXCLUSIVE: Text Messages Show VP Biden and His Wife Colluded to Suppress HUNTER'S ACTIONS WITH A CERTAIN MINOR*. Retrieved from TheGatewayPundit.com: https://www.thegatewaypundit.com/2020/10/breaking-exclusive-text-messages-show-vp-biden-wife-brother-key-family-members-aware-concerned-colluded-suppress-hunters-actions-around-certain-minor/

Hoft, J. (2020, November 25). *BREAKING: KRAKEN RELEASED! Attorney Sidney Powell Files 104 Page BOMBSHELL COMPLAINT of Massive Fraud in Georgia Election – Update: Michigan too*. Retrieved from TheGatewayPundit.com: https://www.thegatewaypundit.com/2020/11/breaking-kraken-released-attorney-sidney-powell-files-104-page-bombshell-complain-massive-fraud-georgia-election/

Hoft, J. (2020, December 11). *BREAKING: US Supreme Court Throws Out Texas Lawsuit Against Pennsylvania, Georgia, Michigan and Wisconsin*. Retrieved from TheGatewayPundit.com: https://www.thegatewaypundit.com/2020/12/

breaking-us-supreme-court-throws-texas-lawsuit-pennsylvania-georgia-michigan-wisconsin/

Hoft, J. (2020, November 5). *Corey Lewandowski: Philly Law Enforcement told Us They WILL NOT Enforce Court Order that Demands Election Observers (VIDEO).* Retrieved from TheGatewayPundit.com: https://www.thegatewaypundit.com/2020/11/corey-lewandowski-philly-law-enforcement-told-us-will-not-enforce-court-order-demands-election-observers-video/

Hoft, J. (2020, October 15). *DAY 2 BOMBSHELL: Newly Released Emails Show How Hunter Biden Worked to Cash in Big on China WITH MONEY HELD FOR HIS DAD, JOE BIDEN!* Retrieved from TheGatewayPundit.com: https://www.thegatewaypundit.com/2020/10/day-2-bombshell-newly-released-emails-show-hunter-biden-worked-cash-big-china-money-held-joe-biden/

Hoft, J. (2020, December 21). *EXCLUSIVE: Carter Page Was Accused of Doing with Russia Exactly What Hunter Biden Did with China.* Retrieved from TheGatewayPundit.com: https://www.thegatewaypundit.com/2020/12/exclusive-carter-page-accused-russia-hunter-biden-china/

Hoft, J. (2020, November 8). *EXCLUSIVE: Detroit Ballot Counters Were Counting "Xerox Copies" as Actual Military Votes (Video).* Retrieved from TheGatewayPundit.com: https://www.thegatewaypundit.com/2020/11/exclusive-detroit-ballot-counters-counting-zerox-copies-actual-military-votes-video/

Hoft, J. (2020, November 20). *HAPPY THANKSGIVING! Lin Wood Announces Sidney Powell Will File Major Lawsuit in Georgia Tomorrow!* Retrieved from TheGatewayPundit.com: https://www.thegatewaypundit.com/2020/11/happy-thanksgiving-lin-wood-announces-sidney-powell-will-file-lawsuit-georgia-tomorrow/

Hoft, J. (2020, December 11). *https:*//www.thegatewaypundit.com/2020/12/gop-minority-leader-kevin-mccarthy-joins-125-house-republicans-supporting-texas-supreme-court-lawsuit-pennsylvania-michigan-georgia-wisconsin/. Retrieved from TheGatewayPundit.com: https://www.thegatewaypundit.com/2020/12/alaska-19th-state-join-amicus-curiae-states-texas-scotus-lawsuit-found-balls/

Hoft, J. (2020, October 29). *HUGE BREAKING EXCLUSIVE: Hunter Biden Has a PornHub Account Where He Uploaded His Personal Porn – Including with Family Member.* Retrieved from TheGatewayPundit.com: https://www.thegatewaypundit.com/2020/10/huge-breaking-exclusive-hunter-biden-porn-hub-account-uploaded-personal-porn-including-family-members/

Hoft, J. (2020, October 28). *Jack Dorsey of Twitter Defends Censoring President Trump but not Iran's America Hating Ayatollah.* Retrieved from TheGatewayPundit.com: https://www.thegatewaypundit.com/2020/10/jack-dorsey-twitter-defends-censoring-president-trump-not-irans-america-hating-ayatollah/

Hoft, J. (2020, December 7). *Obama Judge in Michigan Labels Sidney Powell's Case of Voting Irregularities "An Amalgamation of Theories, Conjecture, and Speculation".* Retrieved from TheGatewayPundit.com: https://www.thegatewaypundit.com/2020/12/obama-judge-michigan-labels-sidney-powells-case-voting-irregularities-amalgamation-theories-conjecture-speculation/

Hoft, J. (2020, November 24). *Pennsylvania, Michigan and Arizona Announce Election Fraud Hearings.* Retrieved from TheGatewayPundit.com: https://www.thegatewaypundit.com/2020/11/pennsylvania-michigan-arizona-announce-election-fraud-hearings/

Hoft, J. (2020, November 26). *President Trump's Dream Team Is the Greatest Assembly of Attorneys in US History Fighting for the Survival of the Nation.* Retrieved from TheGatewayPundit.com: https://www.thegatewaypundit.com/2020/11/president-trumps-dream-team-greatest-assembly-attorneys-us-history-fighting-survival-nation/

Hoft, J. (2020, December 11). *Sidney Powell Announces Emergency Filings in Georgia, Michigan, Arizona and Wisconsin.* Retrieved from TheGatewayPundit.com: https://www.thegatewaypundit.com/2020/12/sidney-powell-announces-emergency-filings-georgia-michigan-arizona-wisconsin/

Hoft, J. (2020, December 13). *Sidney Powell Asks the Supreme Court to Intervene and Decertify States' Results in Michigan, Arizona, Georgia and Wisconsin.* Retrieved from TheGatewayPundit.com: https://www.thegatewaypundit.com/2020/12/sidney-powell-asks-supreme-court-intervene-decertify-states-results-michigan-arizona-georgia-wisconsin/

Hoft, J. (2020, December 8). *Statistician in Texas Lawsuit Against Georgia, Michigan, Pennsylvania and Wisconsin Says Probability of Biden Winning Election Was One in a Quadrillion!* Retrieved from TheGatewayPundit.com: https://www.thegatewaypundit.com/2020/12/statistician-texas-lawsuit-georgia-michigan-pennsylvania-wisconsin-says-probability-biden-winning-election-one-quadrillion/

Hoft, J. (2020, December 8). *Texas Files Lawsuit with Supreme Court Challenging Election Procedures in Georgia, Michigan, Pennsylvania and Wisconsin.* Retrieved from TheGatewayPundit.com: https://www.thegatewaypundit.com/2020/12/texas-files-lawsuit-supreme-court-challenging-election-procedures-georgia-michigan-pennsylvania-wisconsin/

Hoft, J. (2020, December 12). *These Three Trump Judges Threw the President Under the Bus and the Texas Case in The Garbage.* Retrieved from TheGatewayPundit.com: https://www.thegatewaypundit.com/2020/12/three-trump-judges-threw-president-bus-texas-case-garbagety-uphold-constitution/

Hoft, J. (2020, December 9). *UPDATE: 18 States Join Texas in Supreme Court Lawsuit Against Michigan, Georgia, Wisconsin and Pennsylvania Over Fraudulent Election.* Retrieved from TheGatewayPundit.com: https://www.thegatewaypundit.

com/2020/12/update-18-states-join-texas-supreme-court-lawsuit-michigan-georgia-wisconsin-pennsylvania-fraudulent-election/

Hoft, J. (2021, May 28). *'Audit' of Windham, New Hampshire Is a SHAM Due to Conflicts, Independence Issues, and a Ridiculous Audit Program – America Deserves Better.* Retrieved from TheGatewayPundit.com: https://www.thegatewaypundit.com/2021/05/audit-windham-new-hampshire-sham-due-conflicts-independence-issues-ridiculous-audit-program-citizens-new-hampshire-deserve-better/

Hoft, J. (2021, March 6). *After Finding Shredded Ballots in the Dumpster Earlier Today – A Mysterious Fire Breaks Out at Maricopa County Official's Farm.* Retrieved from TheGatewayPundit.com: https://www.thegatewaypundit.com/2021/03/finding-shredded-ballots-dumpster-earlier-today-mysterious-fire-breaks-maricopa-county-officials-farm/

Hoft, J. (2021, June 3). *After Missing Several Days and Putting His Hands In His Pockets When He Was Present, Verified Voting's Mark Lindeman Claims The Windham Audit Was 'Robust'.* Retrieved from TheGatewayPundit.com: https://www.thegatewaypundit.com/2021/06/hardly-showing-putting-hands-pockets-present-verified-votings-mark-lindeman-claims-windham-audit-robust/

Hoft, J. (2021, August 20). *AG Barr Told Lt. Col. Tony Shaffer to Stop Looking Into Truck Driver Jesse Morgan's Testimony That He Moved More Than 200,000 Fraudulent Ballots from NY to PA Before the 2020 Election.* Retrieved from TheGatewayPundit.com: https://www.thegatewaypundit.com/2021/08/ag-barr-told-lt-col-tony-shaffer-stop-looking-truck-driver-jesse-morgans-testimony-moved-200000-fraudulent-ballots-ny-pa-2020-election/

Hoft, J. (2021, May 21). *Antrim County in Michigan, Where First System 'Glitch' In 2020 Election Was Identified, Decides Not to Use Dominion Voting Machines in Upcoming May Election.* Retrieved from TheGatewayPundit.com: https://www.thegatewaypundit.com/2021/03/antrim-county-michigan-first-system-glitch-2020-election-identified-decides-not-use-dominion-voting-machines-upcoming-may-election/

Hoft, J. (2021, June 11). *Arizona Lawmaker Responds to AG Garland: "You Will Not Touch Arizona Ballots or Machines Unless You Want to Spend Time in Arizona Prison".* Retrieved from TheGatewayPundit.com: https://www.thegatewaypundit.com/2021/06/arizona-lawmaker-responds-ag-garland-will-not-touch-arizona-ballots-machines-unless-want-spend-time-arizona-prison/

Hoft, J. (2021, December 28). *Back on June 18 Gateway Pundit Was First to Report on Deep State Plant Ray Epps at the J-6 Protests — Today the Ray Epps Story Finally Made the Mainstream Daily Mail.* Retrieved from TheGatewayPundit.com: https://www.thegatewaypundit.com/2021/12/back-june-18-gateway-pundit-first-report-deep-state-plant-ray-epps-j-6-protests-today-ray-epps-story-finally-made-mainstream-daily-mail/

Hoft, J. (2021, March 6). *BIG NEWS FROM NEW HAMPSHIRE! Secretary of State Gardner Agrees to Forensic Audit of Windham's Voting Machines AND Ballots.* Retrieved from TheGatewayPundit.com: https://www.thegatewaypundit.com/2021/03/big-news-new-hampshire-secretary-state-gardner-agrees-forensic-audit-windhams-voting-machines-ballots/

Hoft, J. (2021, May 26). *BREAKING EXCLUSIVE: The Windham, New Hampshire 2020 Election Audit Was Over Before It Started – Two of Three Auditors Have Conflicts with Pelosi and Schumer.* Retrieved from TheGatewayPundit.com: https://www.thegatewaypundit.com/2021/05/breaking-exclusive-windham-new-hampshire-2020-election-audit-started-two-three-auditors-conflicts-pelosi-schumer/

Hoft, J. (2021, June 15). *BREAKING EXCLUSIVE: UN, US, Facebook and Smartmatic Executives Conspired Together Before the 2020 Election and Many of Same Officials Now Trying to Stop or Derail 2020 Election Audits Taking Place.* Retrieved from TheGatewayPundit.com: https://www.thegatewaypundit.com/2021/06/

breaking-exclusive-un-us-facebook-smartmatic-executives-connived-together-2020-election-now-trying-stop-derail-2020-election-audits-taking-place/

Hoft, J. (2021, April 12). *BREAKING: New Hampshire Governor SIGNS SB 43 INTO LAW! – Mandates Audit of Windham's Fraudulent 2020 Election Results!* Retrieved from TheGatewayPundit.com: https://www.thegatewaypundit.com/2021/04/breaking-new-hampshire-governor-signs-sb-43-law-mandates-audit-windhams-fraudulent-2020-election-results/

Hoft, J. (2021, May 27). *BREAKING: One of Three Auditors Exits Windham, NH Election Audit – Law Requires a Team of Three Auditors.* Retrieved from TheGatewayPundit.com: https://www.thegatewaypundit.com/2021/05/breaking-one-three-auditors-exits-windham-nh-election-audit-law-requires-team-three-auditors/

Hoft, J. (2021, September 30). *BREAKING: THE LIST – Nearly 700,000 Maricopa County Ballots Identified with Issues from the Audit and Separate Canvassing Work to Date.* Retrieved from TheGatewayPundit.com: https://www.thegatewaypundit.com/2021/09/breaking-exclusive-nearly-700000-ballots-arizona-identified-issues-audit-canvassing-work-date/

Hoft, J. (2021, August 25). *Corrupt Obama Judge Orders Lin Wood and Sidney Powell Be Punished for Daring to Sue the State for Election Fraud in the 2020 Election.* Retrieved from TheGatewayPundit.com: https://www.thegatewaypundit.com/2021/08/corrupt-obama-judge-michigan-orders-lin-wood-sidney-powell-punished-daring-sue-state-election-fraud-2020-election/

Hoft, J. (2021, July 18). *Cyber Ninjas Found So Many Issues with the Voting Machines and Processes in Maricopa County It's a Wonder the Previous Auditors Didn't Find These Issues Too.* Retrieved from TheGatewayPundit.com: https://www.thegatewaypundit.com/2021/07/cyber-ninjas-found-many-issues-voting-machines-processes-maricopa-county-wonder-previous-auditors-didnt-find-issues/

Hoft, J. (2021, April 9). *Democrats in Arizona Are Petrified – They're Bringing in Marc Elias's Perkins Coie to Make Threats and Make the Maricopa County Audit Go Away*. Retrieved from TheGatewayPundit.com: https://www.thegatewaypundit.com/2021/04/democrats-arizona-scared-bringing-marc-eliass-perkins-coie-make-threats-make-maricopa-county-audit-go-away/

Hoft, J. (2021, June 29). *Dirtbag Bill Barr Said Driving Vanloads of Ballots into Detroit's TCF Center Late at Night was "Entirely Normal" – Blocking GOP Observers from Counting Room Was Acceptable*. Retrieved from TheGatewayPundit.com: https://www.thegatewaypundit.com/2021/06/dirtbag-bill-barr-said-driving-vanloads-ballots-detroits-tcf-center-later-night-entirely-normal-blocking-gop-observers-counting-room-acceptable/

Hoft, J. (2021, April 27). *EMERGENCY ALERT: Windham, New Hampshire Officials Choose Far-Left Group to Conduct Forensic Audit — PLEASE CONTACT WINDHAM OFFICIALS TODAY!* Retrieved from TheGatewayPundit.com: https://www.thegatewaypundit.com/2021/04/emergency-alert-windham-new-hampshire-officials-may-choose-far-left-group-conduct-forensic-audit-please-contact-state-officials-today/

Hoft, J. (2021, March 13). *FBI Is Looking to Arrest and Abuse 500 More of the 800 Individuals Who Entered the US Capitol on January 6 – Out of the One Million Who Saw Trump Speak*. Retrieved from TheGatewayPundit.com: https://www.thegatewaypundit.com/2021/03/fbi-looking-arrest-abuse-500-800-individuals-entered-us-capitol-january-6-one-million-saw-trump-speak/

Hoft, J. (2021, June 8). *Fraud Cases Shows 87 Total Cases – Trump and/or GOP Won 71% of Cases Where Merits Were Heard*. Retrieved from TheGatewayPundit.com: https://www.thegatewaypundit.com/2021/06/exclusive-accurate-list-2020-election-fraud-cases-shows-87-total-cases-trump-gop-won-71-cases-merits-heard/

Hoft, J. (2021, May 2). *Hey New Hampshire – Look At who 'Verified Voting' (the Firm Selected to Audit Windham) Is Associating With.* Retrieved from TheGatewayPundit.com: https://www.thegatewaypundit.com/2021/05/hey-new-hampshire-look-entities-verified-voting-firm-selected-audit-windham-associating/

Hoft, J. (2021, February 26). *IGNORED BY MEDIA AND FBI: Antifa-BLM Activists Are Posting Photos and Bragging Online About Storming US Capitol on Jan. 6.* Retrieved from TheGatewayPundit.com: https://www.thegatewaypundit.com/2021/02/ignored-media-fbi-antifa-blm-activists-posting-photos-bragging-online-storming-us-capitol-jan-6/

Hoft, J. (2021, July 16). *IT WAS ALL A LIE: Congress Was Evacuated on Jan. 6 Due to Pipe Bomb Threat — Not Because of Trump Supporters Walking Halls.* Retrieved from TheGatewayPundit.com: https://www.thegatewaypundit.com/2021/07/lie-congress-evacuated-jan-6-due-pipe-bomb-threat-not-trump-supporters-walking-halls/

Hoft, J. (2021, February 18). *Maricopa County Audits Are Proving to Be a Waste of Time and Money, They Were Never Created to Identify the Suspected Election Fraud in the County.* Retrieved from TheGatewayPundit.com: https://www.thegatewaypundit.com/2021/02/maricopa-county-audits-proving-waste-time-money-never-created-identify-suspected-election-fraud-county/

Hoft, J. (2021, January 6). *Pence Betrayed General Flynn in 2017 and Today He Betrayed President Trump and America.* Retrieved from TheGatewayPundit.com: https://www.thegatewaypundit.com/2021/01/pence-stabbed-betrayed-general-flynn-2017-today-betrayed-president-trump-america/

Hoft, J. (2021, February 11). *Someone Tell President Trump's Attorneys – The Democrats' Footage Showing Violence at the Capitol on January 6th Was Filmed by Antifa.* Retrieved from TheGatewayPundit.com: https://www.thegatewaypundit.com/2021/02/please-tell-president-trumps-attorneys-democrats-main-footage-showing-violence-capitol-january-6th-filmed-antifa/

Hoft, J. (2021, January 5). *These Seven States Provided Two Sets of Electors to the US Congress – Tomorrow We See How They Will Be Handled.* Retrieved from TheGatewayPundit.com: https://www.thegatewaypundit.com/2021/01/seven-states-provided-two-sets-electors-us-congress-tomorrow-see-will-handled/

Hoft, J. (2021, January 6). *Today In a Matter of Minutes – Vice President Pence Will Become Known in History as a Hero or a Traitor – Which Will It Be?* Retrieved from TheGatewayPundit.com: https://www.thegatewaypundit.com/2021/01/today-matter-minutes-vice-president-will-become-known-history-hero-traitor-will/

Hoft, J. (2021, January 24). *Update on the BIG LIE: Law Professor Confirms Election Fraud Evidence Is "Significant" – Cases Only Dismissed on Process Grounds Not Merit.* Retrieved from TheGatewayPundit.com: https://www.thegateway-pundit.com/2021/01/update-big-lie-law-professor-confirms-election-fraud-evidence-significant-cases-dismissed-process-grounds-not-merit/

Hoft, J. (2021, February 23). *UPDATE: BLM-Antifa Organizer John Sullivan, Who Was Arrested After Storming US Capitol, Bashing Windows Is Writing a Book, Being Paid for Video as Trump Supporters Rot in Jail.* Retrieved from TheGatewayPundit.com: https://www.thegatewaypundit.com/2021/02/update-blm-antifa-organizer-john-sullivan-arrested-storming-us-capitol-bashing-windows-writing-book-paid-video-trump-supporters-rot-jail/

Hoft, J. (2022, March 31). *"Bill Barr Broke the Law... The Fix Is In... Bill Barr Did Not Do His Job" – EXCLUSIVE VIDEO: Tony Shaffer on Barr's Actions After the 2020 Election.* Retrieved from TheGatewayPundit.com: https://www.thegatewaypundit.com/2022/03/breaking-exclusive-bill-barr-broke-law-fix-bill-barr-not-job-tony-shaffer-barrs-actions-2020-election/

Hoft, J. (2022, April 15). *"On that Drive, There Was More than Enough Evidence of Wrongdoing in the Ukraine Under the Previous [Obama] Administration" – Exclusive with John Paul Mac Isaac – Computer Repairman Who Handled Hunter Biden's Laptop*. Retrieved from TheGatewayPundit.com: https://www.thegatewaypundit.com/2022/04/drive-enough-evidence-wrongdoing-ukraine-previous-obama-administration-john-paul-mac-isaac-exclusive-computer-repairman-handled-hunt/

Hoft, J. (2022, May 7). *ARROGANT CORRUPTION: To This Day Georgia's Secretary of State Raffensperger IGNORES Multiple Issues Identified by President Trump's Auditor and Georgia State Senator and former Judge William Ligon from the 2020 Election*. Retrieved from TheGatewayPundit.com: https://www.thegatewaypundit.com/2022/05/arrogant-corruption-day-georgias-secretary-state-raffensperger-ignored-multiple-issues-identified-president-trumps-auditor-georgia-senator-former-judge-william-ligon-fro/

Hoft, J. (2022, May 22). *Attorney David Clements Discusses the 2020 Election Work in New Mexico "Focusing More on the Machine-Driven Aspects of Fraud"*. Retrieved from TheGatewayPundit.com: https://www.thegatewaypundit.com/2022/05/attorney-david-clements-discusses-2020-election-work-new-mexico-focusing-machine-driven-aspects-fraud/

Hoft, J. (2022, September 22). *BARR LIED! FOIA Requests Reveal There Were No DOJ Investigations on Election Fraud After 2020 Election as Bill Barr Claims (VIDEO)*. Retrieved from TheGatewayPundit.com: https://www.thegatewaypundit.com/2022/09/bill-barr-lied-foia-requests-reveal-no-doj-investigations-election-fraud-2020-election-bill-barr-claimed-video/

Hoft, J. (2022, August 11). *BOMBSHELL: Evidence Shows Michigan Supreme Court Race in 2020 Was Flipped – Election Audit Professionals Also Identify Numerous Red Flags in New Mexico and Arizona*. Retrieved from TheGatewayPundit.com: https://www.thegatewaypundit.com/2022/08/bombshell-evidence-shows-michigan-supreme-court-race-2020-flipped-election-audit-professionals-also-identify-numerous-red-flags-new-mexico-arizona/

Hoft, J. (2022, July 8). *BREAKING BIG: Wisconsin Supreme Court Rules Public Absentee Drop Boxes ILLEGAL!* Retrieved from TheGatewayPundit.com: https://www.thegatewaypundit.com/2022/07/breaking-big-wisconsin-supreme-court-rules-absentee-drop-boxes-illegal/

Hoft, J. (2022, December 8). *BREAKING EXCLUSIVE: Daniel Kimmage Deposition By MO and LA AGs Reveals State Department Was Funding Online Fact-Checkers to Censor Speech.* Retrieved from TheGatewayPundit.com: https://www.thegatewaypundit.com/2022/12/breaking-exclusive-deposition-daniel-kimmage-uncovers-state-department-funding-fact-checkers-possibly-us/

Hoft, J. (2022, December 17). *BREAKING EXCLUSIVE: The 2021 Maricopa Audit Proved After Three Days that the 2020 Election in Arizona Was Uncertifiable (Part I).* Retrieved from TheGatewayPundit.com: https://www.thegateway-pundit.com/2022/12/exclusive-truth-behind-2021-maricopa-audit-bal-lot-counting-review-ended-three-days-confirmed-results-uncertifiable/

Hoft, J. (2022, December 17). *BREAKING EXCLUSIVE: The 2021 Maricopa Audit Was a Crime Scene After 3 Days When Every Seal on Every Box Was Found Broken Before Review (Part II).* Retrieved from TheGatewayPundit.com: https://www.thegatewaypundit.com/2022/12/breaking-exclusive-2021-mar-icopa-audit-crime-scene-3-days-every-seal-every-box-found-broken-review-part-ii/

Hoft, J. (2022, December 10). *CAUGHT IN LIES: Latest Twitter Files Release Reveals Feds and Twitter Both Caught Lying, Hiding Evidence in Major Lawsuit; Missouri Attorney General Eric Schmitt Calls Them Onto the Carpet.* Retrieved from TheGatewayPundit.com: https://www.thegatewaypundit.com/2022/12/caught-lies-latest-twitter-files-release-reveals-feds-twitter-caught-lying-hiding-evidence-major-lawsuit-missouri-attorney-general-eric-schmitt-c-alls-onto-carpet/

Hoft, J. (2022, March 20). *Democrats and Dominion Now Trying to Stop 2020 Election Audit in New Mexico – US House Oversight Committee Getting Involved.*

Retrieved from TheGatewayPundit.com: https://www.thegatewaypundit.com/2022/03/democrats-dominion-now-trying-stop-2020-election-audit-new-mexico-us-house-oversight-committee-getting-involved/

Hoft, J. (2022, May 18). *EXCLUSIVE FINDING: Patterns Identified in New Mexico Voter Rolls Are Not Consistent with Random, Human Behavior – What's Going On?* Retrieved from TheGatewayPundit.com: https://www.thegateway-pundit.com/2022/05/exclusive-finding-patterns-identified-new-mexico-voter-rolls-not-consistent-random-human-behavior-going/

Hoft, J. (2022, July 21). *EXCLUSIVE: Radical Far-Left Group (EIP) Created Partnership with Government and Social Media to Censor and Ban Any 2020 Election Reporting – The Gateway Pundit Was Top Target*. Retrieved from TheGatewayPundit.com: https://www.thegatewaypundit.com/2022/07/exclusive-radical-far-left-group-eip-created-partnership-government-social-media-crush-2020-election-reporting-gateway-pundit-top-target/

Hoft, J. (2022, October 28). *EXCLUSIVE: Tuesday's Georgia Supreme Court Ruling Will Likely Lead to Audit of 147,000 Suspected Fraudulent Ballots in Fulton County in the 2020 Election*. Retrieved from TheGatewayPundit.com: https://www.thegatewaypundit.com/2022/10/exclusive-georgia-supreme-court-ruling-likely-will-lead-audit-147000-suspected-fraudulent-ballots-fulton-county-2020-election/

Hoft, J. (2022, December 19). *FBI Paid Twitter $3.4 Million in US Tax Dollars for Administration Costs Related to the Staff's Time Spent Working with the FBI.* Retrieved from TheGatewayPundit.com: https://www.thegatewaypundit.com/2022/12/fbi-paid-twitter-3-4-million-us-tax-dollars-administration-costs-related-staffs-time-spent-working-fbi/

Hoft, J. (2022, January 6). *JAN 6 REMEMBERED: Confirmed: Jan. 6 Protest Resulted in Estimated $1.5 Million in Damages — Or 1/1000th of Damages by Black Lives Matter-Antifa Protests in 2020*. Retrieved from TheGatewayPundit.com:

https://www.thegatewaypundit.com/2022/01/jan-6-remembered-confirmed-jan-6-protest-resulted-estimated-1-5-million-damages-1-1000th-damages-black-lives-matter-antifa-protests-2020/

Hoft, J. (2022, December 24). *Jan 6 Report Hides Any Mention of Pipe Bomber Who Was Cause of Shutting Down Congress That Day.* Retrieved from TheGatewayPundit.com: https://www.thegatewaypundit.com/2022/12/jan-6-report-hides-mention-pipe-bomber-cause-shutting-congress-day/

Hoft, J. (2022, December 4). *Long Before Elon Musk's Disclosure – Dr. Shiva Ayyadurai Uncovered Twitter's "Partner Support Portal" Used by Democrats, Govt. Officials, and Twitter Associates to Censor Conservatives.* Retrieved from TheGatewayPundit.com: https://www.thegatewaypundit.com/2022/12/long-elon-musks-disclosure-dr-shiva-ayyadurai-uncovered-twitters-partner-support-portal-used-democrats-govt-officials-twitter-associates-censor-cons/

Hoft, J. (2022, August 26). *MAJOR UPDATE: Missouri AG Schmitt's Lawsuit FORCES Zuckerberg to ADMIT the FBI TOLD FACEBOOK TO CENSOR THE BIDEN LAPTOP During the 2020 Election.* Retrieved from TheGatewayPundit.com: https://www.thegatewaypundit.com/2022/08/major-update-missouri-ag-schmitts-lawsuit-forces-zuckerberg-admit-fbi-told-facebook-censor-biden-laptop-2020-election/

Hoft, J. (2022, May 2). *Mark Levin on FOX News Calls the Jan 6 Committee "A Front Politburo Type Committee Set Up by Nancy Pelosi…Very Stalinist in its Makeup".* Retrieved from TheGatewayPundit.com: https://www.thegatewaypundit.com/2022/05/mark-levin-fox-news-calls-jan-6-committee-front-politburo-type-committee-set-nancy-pelosi-stalinist-makeup/

Hoft, J. (2022, June 15). *NEVER FORGET: Antifa-BLM Leader Who Was Filmed Inside US Capitol on Jan. 6, Broke a Window, and Organized Antifa Rally Near Capitol That Day – ONLY SPENT ONE DAY IN JAIL.* Retrieved from

TheGatewayPundit.com: https://www.thegatewaypundit.com/2022/06/never-forget-antifa-operative-filmed-inside-us-capitol-jan-6-broke-window-organized-antifa-rally-near-capitol-day-spent-one-day-jail/

Hoft, J. (2022, June 9). *NEVER FORGET: Capitol Police Gassed and Beat Trump Supporter Rosanne Boyland til She Died — Then The Government Cremated Her Body So Her Family Could Not See Her Bloody Wounds*. Retrieved from TheGatewayPundit.com: https://www.thegatewaypundit.com/2022/06/never-forget-capitol-police-gassed-beat-trump-supporter-rosanne-boyland-til-died-government-cremated-body-family-not-see-bloody-wounds/

Hoft, J. (2022, May 11). *SHOCKING: Per New Mexico Auditors Dominion Voting Systems Can Fill-In Ballots – Uncovered 2019 New York State Audit Confirms This*. Retrieved from TheGatewayPundit.com: https://www.thegatewaypundit.com/2022/05/shocking-dominions-voting-systems-can-fill-ballots-noted-new-mexico-auditors-uncovered-2019-new-york-state-audit-confirms/

Hoft, J. (2022). The Steal - Volume I: Setting the Stage. In J. Hoft, *The Steal: Volume I - Setting the Stage* (p. 111). Las Vegas: Joe Hoft.

Hoft, J. (2022, December 24). *Trump Supporters Killed by Police That Day – And Only Mention Ashli Babbitt in Passing – And No Mention of Attempted Murder of Derrick Vargo Who Was Pushed Off 2-Story Ledge by Police*. Retrieved from The: https://www.thegatewaypundit.com/2022/12/jan-6-commission-neglects-mention-3-4-trump-supporters-killed-police-day-mention-ashli-babbitt-passing-no-mention-attempted-murder-derrick-vargo-pushed/

Hoft, J. (2022, December 3). *TWITTER FILES, PT. 2: Documents Reveal Secret Blacklists and Censorship of Conservative Users – Something former Owner Jack Dorsey Said Was Not Happening*. Retrieved from TheGatewayPundit.com: https://www.thegatewaypundit.com/2022/12/twitter-files-pt-2-documents-reveal-secret-blacklists-conservative-users-via-barry-weiss-substack/

Hoft, J. (2022, June 9). *Why Were Ukrainian Nazis in the U.S. Capitol on January 6?* Retrieved from TheGatewayPundit.com: https://www.thegatewaypundit.com/2022/06/ukrainian-nazis-u-s-capitol-january-6/

Hoft, J. (2023, March 15). *"Jan. 6 I Think Is Probably Second Only to the 2020 Election as the Biggest Scam in My Lifetime" – Tucker During Interview with Jan 6 "Political Hostage" Daniel Goodwyn.* Retrieved from TheGatewayPundit.com: https://www.thegatewaypundit.com/2023/03/tucker-reports-on-jan-6-defendant-daniel-goodwyn-who-entered-capitol-for-a-minute-but-now-faces-terrorism-charges-and-one-year-in-prison/

Hoft, J. (2023, March 10). *"This Censorship Industrial Complex is a Growth Industry to the Government" – Rep. Matt Gaetz on Government Funded Censorship of Conservatives.* Retrieved from TheGatewayPundit.com: https://www.thegatewaypundit.com/2023/03/this-censorship-industrial-complex-is-a-growth-industry-to-the-government-rep-matt-gaetz-on-government-funded-censorship-of-conservatives/

Hoft, J. (2023, February 9). *A STAR IS BORN! Rep. Anna Paulina Luna TORCHES Yoel Roth – Exposes Democrat-Big Tech-Government Collusion and Former TWITTER EXECS ARE LEFT SPEECHLESS!* Retrieved from TheGatewayPundit.com: https://www.thegatewaypundit.com/2023/02/star-born-rep-anna-paulina-luna-torches-yoel-roth-exposes-democrat-big-tech-government-collusion-former-twitter-execs-left-speechless/

Hoft, J. (2023, January 7). *Biden Regime Spent Tens of Thousands of Dollars to House Ashli Babbitt's Killer Mike Byrd in Special "Distinguished Visitor Suite" After He Murdered Ashli.* Retrieved from TheGatewayPundit.com: https://www.thegatewaypundit.com/2023/01/biden-regime-spent-tens-thousands-dollars-house-ashli-babbitts-killer-mike-byrd-special-distinguished-visitor-suite-murdered-ashli/

Hoft, J. (2023, April 7). *BOMBSHELL REVELATION: State Department's GEC, Soros's Open Society, the EU, and UK Are Funding the "Disinformation Index": A Pseudo-Nonprofit that "Blacklists" Conservative News from Online Advertisers.* Retrieved from TheGatewayPundit.com: https://www.thegatewaypundit.com/2023/04/bombshell-state-departments-gec-soross-open-society-the-european-union-and-the-uk-are-funding-the-disinformation-index-a-pseudo-nonprofit-that-blacklists-conservative-news-for-adverti/

Hoft, J. (2023, March 6). *BREAKING: Tucker Carlson Releases Video Showing Capitol Police Escorting Jacob Chansley "QAnon Shaman" Peacefully Through the Capitol (VIDEO).* Retrieved from TheGatewayPundit.com: https://www.thegatewaypundit.com/2023/03/breaking-tucker-carlson-releases-video-showing-capitol-police-escorting-jacob-chansley-qanon-shaman-peacefully-through-the-capitol/

Hoft, J. (2023, February 28). *Court Documents Detail How Paul Ryan Pushed FOX News Owners to "Move on from Trump" Despite Polls Showing Channel Was Losing Its Core Viewers.* Retrieved from TheGatewayPundit.com: https://www.thegatewaypundit.com/2023/02/court-documents-detail-how-paul-ryan-pushed-fox-news-owners-to-move-on-from-trump-despite-polls-showing-channel-was-losing-its-core-viewers/

Hoft, J. (2023, April 19). *EXCLUSIVE: Corrupt Senator Mark Warner's "Restrict Act" Is the Patriot Act for Elections that Gives the Government Enormous Power – Forcing Counties to Enable "Albert Sensors" or Mandate Other Sinister Election Activities.* Retrieved from TheGatewayPundit.com: https://www.thegatewaypundit.com/2023/04/exclusive-corrupt-senator-mark-warners-restrict-act-is-the-patriot-act-for-elections-that-give-the-government-enormous-power-forcing-counties-to-enable-albert-sensors-or-mandate-other-sin/

Hoft, J. (2023, April 12). *EXCLUSIVE: Far-Left NGO 'Democracy Fund' Financed Efforts to Certify "Non-Voting Technology" and Use It to Monitor Elections on a Real-Time Basis.* Retrieved from TheGatewayPundit.com: https://www.

thegatewaypundit.com/2023/04/exclusive-far-left-ngo-democracy-fund-funded-effort-to-certify-non-voting-technology-and-use-it-to-monitor-elections-on-a-real-time-basis/

Hoft, J. (2023, February 23). *EXPLOSIVE NEW VIDEO of Rosanne Boyland Shows Police Attempting to Revive Her in Trash-Filled Hall, Police Say She Was "Trampled" – Then Later They Lied and Said She Died of Overdose (VIDEO)*. Retrieved from TheGatewayPundit.com: https://www.thegatewaypundit.com/2023/02/explosive-new-video-of-rosanne-boyland-shows-police-attempting-to-revive-her-in-trash-filled-hall-say-she-was-trampled-then-later-they-lied-and-said-she-died-of-overdose-video/

Hoft, J. (2023, March 14). *EXPLOSIVE: The 2020 Election Steal Required an "Emergency" on Jan 6 to Complete the Coup*. Retrieved from TheGatewayPundit.com: https://www.thegatewaypundit.com/2023/03/explosive-the-2020-election-steal-required-an-emergency-on-jan-6-to-culminate-the-coup/

Hoft, J. (2023, March 17). *HE HAS THE PROOF: DC Gulag Political Prisoner and Decorated Army Special Forces Soldier Jeffrey McKellop Reveals Extent of Government Agents at J6 Capitol Protest – IT WAS A COMPLETE SET-UP! (Audio)*. Retrieved from TheGatewayPundit: https://www.thegatewaypundit.com/2023/03/he-has-the-proof-dc-gulag-political-prisoner-and-decorated-army-special-forces-soldier-jeffrey-mckellop-reveals-extent-of-government-agents-at-j6-capitol-protest-it-was-a-complete-set-up-audio/

Hoft, J. (2023, March 15). *HUGE: "THEY LIED ABOUT EVERYTHING" – 96-Page DC Police Report UNCOVERED – Shows Govt Knew MAGA Was Coming on Jan 6 and Entrapped Them ALL*. Retrieved from TheGatewayPundit.com: https://www.thegatewaypundit.com/2023/03/huge-they-lied-about-everything-a-96-page-dc-police-report-uncovered-shows-govt-knew-maga-was-coming-on-jan-6-and-entrapped-them-all/

Hoft, J. (2023, February 24). *JEROME CORSI: Obama Went After General Flynn Because He Was a Risk of Indicting Him and Hillary for High Crimes and Misdemeanors (PART 2).* Retrieved from TheGatewayPundit.com: https://www.thegatewaypundit.com/2023/02/jerome-corsi-obama-went-after-general-flynn-because-he-was-a-risk-of-indicting-him-and-hillary-for-high-crimes-and-misdemeanors-part-2/

Hoft, J. (2023, February 11). *NYT Reports On Missouri-Louisiana Lawsuit featuring Gateway Pundit and Esteemed US Doctors Against Government Officials and Agencies Who Censored Our Speech As Lawsuit Comes to a Head.* Retrieved from TheGatewayPundit.com: https://www.thegatewaypundit.com/2023/02/nyt-reports-missouri-louisiana-lawsuit-featuring-gateway-pundit-esteemed-us-doctors-government-officials-agencies-censored-speech-lawsuit-comes-head/

Hoft, J. (2023, March 13). *Ray Epps Lied – He Committed Criminal Acts and It Was ALL CAUGHT on Video — Here Are the Eight Trump Supporters the FBI Arrested and Who Are Serving Years in Prison for Committing Same Act.* Retrieved from TheGatewayPundit.com: https://www.thegatewaypundit.com/2023/03/ray-epps-lied-he-committed-criminal-acts-and-it-was-all-caught-on-video-here-are-the-eight-trump-supporters-who-are-serving-years-in-prison-for-committing-same-crime/

Hoft, J. (2023, March 13). *Soros-Backed NM SOS Caught Lying to Legislature – NM Election System Completely Exposed to the Internet.* Retrieved from TheGatewayPundit.com: https://www.thegatewaypundit.com/2023/03/soros-backed-nm-sos-caught-lying-to-legislature-nm-election-system-completely-exposed-to-the-internet/

Hoft, J. (2023, March 29). *State-Wide Top-Down System" Used in Multiple States Is Internet Connected, Non-Certified, Connects with Dominion and ERIC, and Allows "Plug-Ins" That Can Change Results – And No One Has Reported on This Until Now.* Retrieved from TheGatewayPundit.com: https://www.thegatewaypundit.

com/2023/03/bpros-totalvote-centralized-state-wide-top-down-system-used-in-multiple-states-is-internet-connected-non-certified-connects-with-dominion-and-eric-and-allows-plug-ins-that-can-change-resu/

Hoft, J. (2023, January 6). *Tucker Carlson Discusses Relentless Media Lies About Jan 6 Protests on Second Anniversary of Historic Day.* Retrieved from TheGatewayPundit.com: https://www.thegatewaypundit.com/2023/01/tucker-carlson-discusses-lies-jan-6-relentless-past-two-years/

Integrity, E. (2023, February 10). *Election Integrity.* Retrieved from ElectionIntegrity. org: https://election-integrity.info/

Johnson, L. (2021, September 25). *ENCLOSED: List of Intel Fools Who Pushed Hunter Biden Russian Laptop Lie.* Retrieved from TheGatewayPundit.com: https://www.thegatewaypundit.com/2021/09/enclosed-list-intel-fools-pushed-hunter-biden-russian-laptop-lie/

Kat Lonsdorf, C. D. (2022, June 9). *A timeline of how the Jan. 6 attack unfolded — including who said what and when.* Retrieved from NPR.org: https://www.npr.org/2022/01/05/1069977469/a-timeline-of-how-the-jan-6-attack-unfolded-including-who-said-what-and-when

KNOWiNK.com. (2023, May 8). *Product Suite.* Retrieved from Knowink.com: https://knowink.com/knowink-product-suite/

Laco, K. (2022, May 5). *Lawsuit filed against Biden, top officials for 'colluding' with Big Tech to censor speech on Hunter, COVID.* Retrieved from FoxNews.com: https://www.foxnews.com/politics/lawsuit-filed-against-biden-top-officials-colluding-big-tech-censor-speech-hunter-covid

Laila, C. (2020, December 30). *"This Stops Right Now!"– Rudy Giuliani Testifies on Election Fraud, Urges Georgia Lawmakers to Take Action #StopTheSteal (VIDEO).* Retrieved from TheGatewayPundit.com: https://www.thegatewaypundit.

com/2020/12/stops-right-now-rudy-giuliani-testifies-election-fraud-urges-georgia-lawmakers-take-action-stopthesteal-video/

Laila, C. (2020, December 10). *106 House Republicans Sign Brief Backing Texas Supreme Court Lawsuit Against Pennsylvania, Michigan, Georgia and Wisconsin.* Retrieved from TheGatewayPundit.com: https://www.thegatewaypundit.com/2020/12/106-house-republicans-sign-brief-backing-texas-supreme-court-lawsuit-pennsylvania-michigan-georgia-wisconsin/

Laila, C. (2020, November 30). *Arizona Witness: Truck Loads of Ballots Kept Coming in For 10 Days After Elections Officials Thought They Were Done Counting Votes (VIDEO).* Retrieved from TheGatewayPundit.com: https://www.thegatewaypundit.com/2020/11/arizona-witness-truck-loads-ballots-kept-coming-10-days-elections-officials-thought-done-counting-votes-video/

Laila, C. (2020, October 27). *BREAKING: Hunter Biden Audio Confesses Partnership with China 'Spy Chief' — Joe Biden Named as Witness in SDNY Criminal Case #LaptopFromHell.* Retrieved from TheGatewayPundit.com: https://www.thegatewaypundit.com/2020/10/breaking-hunter-biden-audio-confesses-partnership-china-spy-chief-joe-biden-named-witness-sdny-criminal-case-laptopfromhell/

Laila, C. (2020, November 30). *Dr. Shiva Presents Data at Arizona Hearing That Completely Obliterates Biden Victory Narrative (VIDEO).* Retrieved from TheGatewayPundit.com: https://www.thegatewaypundit.com/2020/11/dr-shiva-presents-data-arizona-hearing-completely-obliterates-biden-victory-narrative-video/

Laila, C. (2020, November 25). *Giuliani Points Out Major Problem with Mail-In Ballots in Pennsylvania: Only 1.8 Mail-In Ballots Were Sent Out – But 2.5 Million Were Counted (VIDEO).* Retrieved from TheGatewayPundit.com: https://www.thegatewaypundit.com/2020/11/giuliani-points-major-problem-mail-ballots-pennsylvania-1-8-mail-ballots-sent-2-5-million-counted-video/

Laila, C. (2020, December 11). *GOP Minority Leader Kevin McCarthy Joins 125 House Republicans in Supporting Texas Supreme Court Lawsuit Against Pennsylvania, Michigan, Georgia and Wisconsin.* Retrieved from TheGatewayPundit.com: https://www.thegatewaypundit.com/2020/12/gop-minority-leader-kevin-mccarthy-joins-125-house-republicans-supporting-texas-supreme-court-lawsuit-pennsylvania-michigan-georgia-wisconsin/

Laila, C. (2020, November 24). *JUST IN: Pennsylvania Secretary of State Certifies Election Results.* Retrieved from TheGatewayPundit.com: https://www.thegatewaypundit.com/2020/11/just-pennsylvania-secretary-state-certifies-election-results/

Laila, C. (2020, November 30). *President Trump Calls Into Hearing on Voting Irregularities in Arizona, Blasts RINO Gov. Doug Ducey (VIDEO).* Retrieved from TheGatewayPundit.com: https://www.thegatewaypundit.com/2020/11/president-trump-calls-hearing-voting-irregularities-arizona-video/

Laila, C. (2020, December 10). *President Trump Files Motion to Join Texas Supreme Court Lawsuit Against Pennsylvania, Michigan, Wisconsin and Georgia.* Retrieved from TheGatewayPundit.com: https://www.thegatewaypundit.com/2020/12/president-trump-files-motion-join-texas-supreme-court-lawsuit/

Laila, C. (2021, January 6). *BREAKING: Pence Releases Statement Ahead of Certification of Electoral College, Says He Will NOT Block Biden's Electors.* Retrieved from TheGatewayPundit.com: https://www.thegatewaypundit.com/2021/01/breaking-pence-releases-statement-ahead-certification-electoral-college-says-will-not-block-bidens-electors/

Laila, C. (2021, January 6). *BREAKING: Pence Releases Statement Ahead of Certification of Electoral College, Says He Will NOT Block Biden's Electors.* Retrieved from TheGatewayPundit.com: https://www.thegatewaypundit.com/2021/01/breaking-pence-releases-statement-ahead-certification-electoral-college-says-will-not-block-bidens-electors/

Laila, C. (2021, July 21). *New: GOP Leader McCarthy Pulls His 5 Republican Members From Jan. 6 Committee After Pelosi Rejects Jordan, Banks*. Retrieved from TheGatewayPundit.com: https://www.thegatewaypundit.com/2021/07/new-gop-leader-mccarthy-pulls-5-republican-members-jan-6-committee-pelosi-rejects-jordan-banks/

Laila, C. (2022, December 2). *BREAKING: HERE IT IS: Elon Musk Reveals Why Twitter Suppressed Hunter Biden 'Laptop From Hell' Story*. Retrieved from TheGatewayPundit.com: https://www.thegatewaypundit.com/2022/12/breaking-elon-musk-reveals-twitter-suppressed-hunter-biden-laptop-story/

Laila, C. (2022, December 9). *BREAKING: Twitter Files Part 3 Released: How Trump Was Removed From Twitter*. Retrieved from TheGatewayPundit.com: https://www.thegatewaypundit.com/2022/12/breaking-twitter-files-trump-removed-twitter-2/

Laila, C. (2022, December 24). *JUST IN: Another Twitter Files Drop: Twitter and "Other Government Agencies"*. Retrieved from TheGatewayPundit.com: https://www.thegatewaypundit.com/2022/12/just-another-twitter-files-drop-twitter-government-agencies/

Laila, C. (2022, May 5). *Republican Attorneys General Sue Joe Biden For Colluding with Big Tech to Censor Information on Hunter's 'Laptop From Hell' and Covid*. Retrieved from TheGatewayPundit.com: https://www.thegatewaypundit.com/2022/05/republican-attorneys-general-sue-joe-biden-colluding-big-tech-censor-information-hunters-laptop-covid/

Laila, C. (2023, January 13). *JUST IN: Another 'Twitter Files' Drop: More Adam Schiff Ban Requests – Twitter "Deamplified" Alleged Conservative Accounts They Say Were Linked to Q-Anon*. Retrieved from TheGatewayPundit.com: https://www.thegatewaypundit.com/2023/01/just-another-twitter-files-drop-adam-schiff-ban-requests/

Laila, C. (2023, March 9). *Matt Taibbi Drops Another Twitter Files Ahead of Testimony to Congress: The Censorship-Industrial Complex*. Retrieved from TheGatewayPundit.com: https://www.thegatewaypundit.com/2023/03/matt-taibbi-drops-another-twitter-files-ahead-of-testimony-to-congress-the-censorship-industrial-complex/

Lemon, J. (2020, October 15). *The New York Post's Hunter Biden Stories Raise Questions About Joe Biden and Its Reporting — Here Are 9*. Retrieved from Newsweek.com: https://www.newsweek.com/new-york-posts-hunter-biden-stories-raise-questions-about-joe-biden-its-reporting-here-are-9-1539463

Lupo, B. (2022, December 20). *BREAKING: Georgia Supreme Court Reverses 2020 Election Case Dismissal for "Lack of Standing"…Sent Back to Lower Courts*. Retrieved from TheGatewayPundit.com: https://www.thegatewaypundit.com/2022/12/breaking-georgia-supreme-court-reverses-2020-election-case-dismissal-lack-standing-sent-back-lower-courts/

Mangan, K. B. (2020, December 7). *Federal judge dismisses Sidney Powell lawsuit that sought to overturn Trump loss in Georgia*. Retrieved from CNBC.com: https://www.cnbc.com/2020/12/07/judge-dismisses-sidney-powell-lawsuit-challenging-trump-georgia-loss.html

McMurray, P. (2021, March 6). *BREAKING: Antrim County Clerk and Material Witness, Sheryl Guy, DISMISSES Election Fraud Case – Judge Overrules Her Decision – Reinstates Case*. Retrieved from TheGatewayPundit.com: https://www.thegatewaypundit.com/2021/03/breaking-antrim-county-clerk-material-witness-sheryl-guy-dismisses-election-fraud-casejudge-overrules-decision-reinstates-case/

Murray, J. M. (2021, June 24). *Giuliani is under scrutiny in Georgia probe into Trump*. Retrieved from CNN.com: https://www.cnn.com/2022/06/24/politics/giuliani-georgia-grand-jury-probe-trump/index.html

Naylor, B. (2021, February 10). *Read Trump's Jan. 6 Speech, A Key Part Of Impeachment Trial.* Retrieved from NPR.org: https://www.npr.org/2021/02/10/966396848/read-trumps-jan-6-speech-a-key-part-of-impeachment-trial

Press, A. (2021, February 22). *Supreme Court formally rejects Trump election challenge cases.* Retrieved from NBCNews.com: https://www.nbcnews.com/politics/2020-election/supreme-court-formally-rejects-trump-election-challenge-cases-n1258520

Robertson, K. (2020, October 18). *New York Post Published Hunter Biden Report Amid Newsroom Doubts.* Retrieved from NYTimes. com: https://www.nytimes.com/2020/10/18/business/media/new-york-post-hunter-biden.html

Scoop, T. R. (2020, December 2). *BREAKING: Sidney Powell files NEW lawsuit in Arizona alleging 412k illegal ballots.* Retrieved from TheRightScoop.com: https://therightscoop.com/breaking-sidney-powell-files-new-lawsuit-in-arizona-alleging-412k-illegal-ballots/

Sekulow, J. (2023, February 9). *Jay Sekulow.* Retrieved from JaySekulow.com: https://jaysekulow.com/

Smith, T. (2021, July 9). *CONFIRMED: DC Mayor Bowser and Nancy Pelosi Turned Down THOUSANDS Of National Guard Troops At The Capitol On January 6th.* Retrieved from LaunchLiberty.com: https://launchliberty.com/confirmed-dc-mayor-bowser-and-nancy-pelosi-turned-down-thousands-of-national-guard-troops-at-the-capitol-on-january-6th/

Swoyer, A. (2020, December 9). *Sidney Powell Arizona election lawsuit dismissed by federal judge.* Retrieved from WashingtonTimes.com: https://www.washingtontimes.com/news/2020/dec/9/sidney-powell-arizona-election-lawsuit-dismissed-f/

Thomsen, J. (2021, August 25). *Judge declines to sanction lawyer Sidney Powell in Wisconsin 2020 election case.* Retrieved from Reuters.com: https://www.reuters.com/legal/legalindustry/judge-declines-sanction-lawyer-sidney-powell-wisconsin-2020-election-case-2022-08-25/

Trump, P. D. (2020, December 19). *RealDonaldTrump.* Retrieved from Twitter.com: https://www.thetrumparchive.com/?searchbox=%22will+be+wild%21%22

University, C. (2023, March 13). *Dr. John Eastman.* Retrieved from Chapman.edu: https://www.chapman.edu/our-faculty/john-eastman

Vlamis, K. (2020, December 10). *Sidney Powell's 'Kraken' lawsuits failed again, as judges in Michigan, Georgia, Arizona, and Wisconsin have now dismissed her cases.* Retrieved from BusinessInsider.com: https://www.businessinsider.com/sidney-powell-lawsuits-dismissed-michigan-georgia-arizona-wisconsin-2020-12?amp

Ward, D. K. (2020, December 5). *The 2020 election was #NonTransparent by force. #Bullying to cheat. #StopTheSteal.* Retrieved from Twitter.com: https://twitter.com/kelliwardaz/status/1335225504899739649?ref_src=twsrc%5Etfw%7Ctwcamp%5Etweetembed%7Ctwterm%5E1335225504899739649%7Ctwgr%5E54d215c133ebfa54194bbfb8de1a3efc3cf94248%7Ctwcon%5Es1_&ref_url=https%3A%2F%2Fwww.thegatewaypundit.com%2F2020%2F12%

Warner, S. M. (2023, March 7). *S686 - RESTRICT Act.* Retrieved from Congress.gov: https://www.congress.gov/bill/118th-congress/senate-bill/686/text?s=1&r=15

Watch, I. (2023, February 10). *65 Project.* Retrieved from InfluenceWatch.org: https://www.influencewatch.org/organization/65-project/

Week, U. L. (2020, December 9). *Sidney Powell's 'Kraken' Voter Fraud Suit Tossed in Arizona (1)*. Retrieved from BloombergLaw.com: https://news.bloomberglaw.com/us-law-week/sidney-powells-kraken-voter-fraud-suit-dismissed-in-arizona

Wikipedia. (2023, February 5). *Cover-up*. Retrieved from Wikipedia: https://en.wikipedia.org/wiki/Cover-up

William Cummings, J. G. (2021, January 6). *By the numbers: President Donald Trump's failed efforts to overturn the election*. Retrieved from USAToday.com: https://www.usatoday.com/in-depth/news/politics/elections/2021/01/06/trumps-failed-efforts-overturn-election-numbers/4130307001/

Zhou, L. (2021, January 7). *147 Republican lawmakers still objected to the election results after the Capitol attack*. Retrieved from Vox.com: https://www.vox.com/2021/1/6/22218058/republicans-objections-election-results

INDEX

ABOUT THE AUTHOR

Joe Hoft is a best-selling author and a radio host at TNTRadio.live. He's contributed at The Gateway Pundit and other conservative websites and he is the creator of many exclusive reports at his own website – www.joehoft.com. Before 2020, Joe was an international corporate executive focusing primarily on finance, operations, IT, and audit. Joe traveled the world during his professional career and attended and presented at corporate board and audit committees in multiple countries.

At one point in his career, Hoft oversaw the financial reporting for billion-dollar and multimillion-dollar entities. After that, he landed in Hong Kong and called that home for nearly a decade. As a corporate executive in Hong Kong, he oversaw a regional audit team in multiple countries across the Asia Pacific region.

Joe Hoft's knowledge gained from decades of audit, finance, operational, and IT work was instrumental in reviewing, analyzing, and putting together this body of work: *The Steal - Volume III: The Cover-Up*. He is the only experienced and fair-minded international audit executive to address the 2020 Election.

Joe has been labeled the "man who first exposed the COVID-19 hoax" for his insights early in the COVID crisis.[280] He's been instrumental in uncovering the lies behind the 2020 Election and can see things before others do.

Joe has appeared on numerous shows on numerous media outlets, and he has interviewed conservative icons including President Trump.

Joe has earned ten degrees and/or designations and has authored five previous books, including most recently *The Steal - Volume I: Setting the Stage* and *The Steal - Volume II: The Impossible Occurs.*

You can follow and reach Joe Hoft at www.joehoft.com.

280 Hoft J., TGP's Joe Hoft "The Man Who First Exposed the COVID-19 Hoax" says NY Gov Cuomo "Should be Investigated and Looked at for Murder" on Infowars (VIDEO), 2020.

Printed in Great Britain
by Amazon

43777572R00099